March 03

With love To Jessie.

From Katie Ross (Mackinnin)

D1424363

A Pillar of Faith

of

Faith

Themes from the Psalms

National Library of Canada Cataloguing in Publication

MacKinnon, Angus Matheson, 1932
    A pillar of faith / Angus Matheson MacKinnon.

ISBN 0-9698337-8-4

1. Bible. O.T. Psalms--Devotional use. I. Title.

BS1451.M3196 2003   242'.5
C2003-900066-4

A Pillar of Faith

Themes from the Psalms

Angus Matheson MacKinnon

THE
CATALONE
PRESS

Printed by City Printers Ltd., Sydney, NS
Cover Design by Harve Grant

Cover Picture:

Seine-netters in Uig Bay, Isle of Skye similar to Alick
MacRae's boat, the Catherine. The black boat is the Gift
which I recommissioned in Stornoway.

AMK

The Catalone Press
P.O. Box 1878
Sydney, NS
B1P 6W4
Canada

Contents

Books by the same author

<u>Devotional</u>
A Dream Come True
Shopping for the Soul
The Cape of Joy
Free to Go

•

Atlantic Challenge
Highland Minister

Introduction

This book in the series Devotional Themes on the Psalms begins with what might be called a finished product— a brief sketch of a devout Christian from Lochcarron in Wester Ross, Scotland.

Lochcarron is historically noted for its contribution to the professions. We lay special value on those ministers who served the Lord there, and those who were raised there to serve the Lord at home and abroad. But apart from ministers there were men and women who witnessed faithfully to the Evangel, and whose lives gave a texture to the community as part of God's vineyard in which many experienced the fragrance of the Master's presence.

Such have an immortality shared with all whose destiny is sealed in the Covenant of Mercy. At the same time, it is right to perpetuate their memory where possible so that here and there generations to come will be influenced to emulate them and serve as Pillars of Faith in the house of God.

One such was Alick MacRae of Lochcarron

Angus MacKinnon
Arnish, Cape Breton, Nova Scotia.

Why read the books in this Series?

One answer is that most religious people are controlled by institutions, Christian, non-Christian, secular atheist or anarchist. They all have one thing in common, they want to take over your life and do your religious thinking for you. Your life is the temple of God's Spirit. Do not sell your soul to any one or any other group of people.

This book is designed for those who think for themselves. It takes control of your life out of the hands of other people. You will not then be exploited by peer pressure, or timidly accept the dictates and decisions of power blocs, religious or secular. Read it and your life will be freed from the control of other people.

Start enjoying thinking for yourself.

Begin using your own faculties of daily prayer, and medition and time. It will strengthen your will, and a tremendous sense of optimism and hope will give you zest for every new day.

Your desires will be drawn to Christ, so that you will be ruled by God and rule with God.

The lines of communication between you and heaven will be open. And God's Spirit will flow through you, bringing a therapy of exquisite well-being in soul, heart, mind and body.

Stress will change to vibrant energy of everlasting love, joy and peace, which in turn will make you a blessing to others.

Higher aims, noble purposes will displace, selfishness, self-centredness and self-pleasing.

A Pillar of the Faith

Alick MacRae was one of the best-known men in Wester Ross. He was a leading elder in Lochcarron Free Church. Truly his life was a wonderful balance of the physical and spiritual. In both he was fearless and diligent. Both were an expression of his faith. Lesser men might think of him as a stern legalist who took his religion too literally. The fact is that his life from one Sabbath to another was one of simple consistency, the life of an unwavering faith and faithful follower of Christ.

On his demobilization, this World War Two soldier determined to make his livelihood as a fisherman. He had a new seine-netter built, hired a crew and fished the west coast, pairing his boat, the Catherine, with that of the MacLeod brothers from Scalpay, Harris, for the Minch herring season. He was a man of clear unclouded conviction that Christ was first in all things, and must 'in all things have the pre-eminence.' (Colossians 1:18) How uninformed we are about the lives of one another! How superficial and hasty are the judgments we make against those who appear to differ from what we think! Men like Alick MacRae convict us because they show us up for what we are not, and ought to be. He served his Lord in both word and deed.

I remember him in different ways. Three occasions are fixed in my memory. First, when I was precenting at a communion in Plockton Free Church, Alick was there in front of me in the middle of the congregation. He looked so stern, the epitome of the strict unbending character associated with severity and spiritual policemanship.

My second impression of him was so different. While crossing the Minch from Stornoway to Kyle of Lochalsh, we shared company and conversation in the wheelhouse of his fishing boat, the Catherine. There was a considerable sea running. We had plenty time to get to know each other before the dawn broke. We called in at Portree to unship a young boy, Kenneth, son of Rev Norman MacLeod, Portree, and grandson of Rev. Kenneth MacRae, Stornoway.

We sang a psalm, read the Word and knelt down on our knees in prayer in the focs'le. That clinched it. There was no divide between us. We were on the same wavelength and the fragrance of the Master and the liberty of the Spirit, felt in that sweet worship round the Word of life was testimony to the Divine benediction on Alick MacRae's life.

Then there was the third occasion. A mutual friend, a marine engineer, Duncan MacPherson, was walking with me on the quay in Stornoway one morning, when I was recommissioning a fishing boat, the Gift previously owned by some Ness fishermen. Several boats were unloading their catch of herring. Duncan, a Skyeman was a seeker who had not found lasting peace in his heart. Sometimes he gave vent to hasty opinions on the lives of positive believers like Alick MacRae. It is also true that many passed judgment on himself unfairly as well.

Suddenly Duncan tugged at my arm. We both stopped. 'Look' he said, his voice like a whisper. He seemed almost in shock, as if something had come over him. He repeated, as one in a trance, 'Look. That's Alick MacRae.'

10

I looked along the quay past the boats. There was Alick MacRae. In silence, we watched him as he left his fishing boat carrying two large white pails full of herring. We watched him. He made his way past several people, past a truck. Our eyes followed his course until he stopped at a door. Above was the sign, Seamen's Mission. This man's faith was not in word only but backed up in deeds. And there was no doubt that his witness that morning had a powerful effect upon Duncan MacPherson.

I like to think, when I finish my course here and come into the last port, that I will not only see my Lord, but also the face of these two friends, so different in many ways, yet who will be there through the opened door of God's mercy and the Resurrection power of Divine love.

"Him that overcometh will I make a pillar in the temple of my God"

Revelation 3:12

Psalm 2

1. Why do the heathen rage, and the people imagine a vain thing?

2. The kings of the earth set themselves, and the rulers take counsel together, against the Lord, and against his anointed, saying, Let us break their bands asunder, and cast away their cords from us.

3. He that sits in heaven shall laugh: the Lord shall have them in derision.

4. Then shall he speak to them in his wrath, and vex them in his sore displeasure.

5. Yet have I set my king on my holy hill of Zion.

6. I will declare the decree: the Lord hath said unto me, Thou art my Son; this day have I begotten thee.

7. Ask of me, and I shall give thee the heathen for thine inheritance, and the uttermost parts of the earth for thy possession.

8. Thou shalt break them with a rod of iron; thou shalt dash them in pieces like a potter's vessel.

9. Be wise now therefore, O ye kings: be instructed, ye judges of the earth.

10. Serve the Lord with fear, and rejoice with trembling.

11. Kiss ye the Son, lest he be angry, and ye perish from the way, when his wrath is kindled but a little. Blessed are all they that put their trust in him.

The Dominion of Christ

Psalm 2 represents a prelude to great things. We say this because even as we stop to dwell upon it, we realise that we are being introduced to the whole Book of Psalms, which is none other than the believer's shopping market. In the first psalm, the journey of the believer is illustrated as a pilgrimage of obedience to the Law of God, a road to heaven, cut through the rocky terrain of a hostile world, over hill and valley, through swollen rivers, and peoples entrenched in alien philosophies, yet at last leading to glory. In this psalm before us we are introduced to the sublime exaltation of the Son, the King of kings. The first speaks of the King's highway, holiness; the second speaks of the King himself.

Now we see the Son presented with the authoritative commission from the Father. In the context of a world view, co-extensive with the universe, we are called to identify this Hebrew psalm as a song of praise to the Jew from Galilee, Jesus of Nazareth. For he is the Son born into our local history of time; he is the King of all kings and governments, to whom the Father has given all authority in heaven and in earth.

If you want to have your heart filled with joy, let your mind dwell upon Psalm Two. Even as you do so, God's Spirit will come upon the Word and upon you as you identify with it. The

Spirit must come upon you so that the Word and your soul meet. You then become part of the communication with heaven. It does not matter about the past, what you did, where you were, what you then wanted, what you worked for. That is behind you. Now you are in a situation of infinite possibilities, where happiness is inevitable, where tears are for your own confessed unworthiness but are dried by God himself with the whispered words of pardon that are written in his Word for the penitent, and spoken to you as you kneel at the Throne of Mercy.

This is the prelude to devotions, a life from now on where you meet daily with your Master and Redeemer, where your soul is given the elixir of forgiveness, and the heart is now furnished with the unqualified allegiance of a faith placed in the Living God. Faith believes in facts, even though unseen. Devotion is the effect of proximity to the Lord. The devotions become stronger as a compelling influence upon our whole life as we dwell upon Christ and the Unsearchable Riches of his Grace. These are displayed in the Psalms to nourish and strengthen our faith, and make us joyful on our journey to Zion.

You see the point, Psalm One gives the formula-- the law of God which is like a road through this world. Psalm Two gives us the Person of the Saviour, the Son of God, the Friend that leads us through all circumstances, to travel on the Way of Holiness. For he is the Way. By our accepting this, our spiritual communion with God has a factual context of history, and Christ is central, as God our Redeemer, touchable for all humans, because he is both the Son of God and the Son of Man. And here our devotions centre round Christ as the King whose Kingdom at last will be established to last for all ages to come.

Do not think that this a reality only in the subjective experience of belief. The psalms reflect history, the unfolding of God's purposes, the transition of the great architect's blueprint into the three-dimensional structure of a renewed world where spirit, mind and matter comprise the integrated unity of God's fulfilled decree. Beyond our personal consciousness of which our belief, our faith in Christ, is one of a myriad testimonies that are linked to the history of mankind, there is the history of Christ's church, which he has purchased for himself with his own blood. Like a great caravan, so the church's passage in time and history, is continually being monitored and plotted by heaven itself, on the graph of God's omnipotence and omniscience. If you listen, you will not only hear the voice of God speaking, and know that he is God: but also if you are very still, you will hear the footsteps of the church, like a mighty army, of those who march towards Zion. If all were in step, the earth would tremble. When all are in step in the unity of one mind and one heart and one will, or wherever there is this, in a great crowd or a little prayer-meeting, the earth trembles, the world retreats, for the Spirit of God dominates, and 'the glory of the Lord fills the tabernacle.'

If the eyes of our understanding are opened, to behold the royal law of life, so our eyes should be open to behold in a real awareness, the great cloud of witnesses who across the centuries, walk in the light, as the children and heirs of God's kingdom.

Do you see? Here is the objective. Here are facts. The individual comes to this phenomenon, and in his or her response to God's call, becomes part of this glorious dimension where we have a progressive society of righteousness which at last will comprise the new world or the renewed world.

Faith rests on the unseen, but unseen facts. The person who steps over a river bank in the dark, where there is no bridge can hardly expect to get safely across the river, however much faith he has. But the Christian steps forward in the dark and his feet find the bridge of Christ's Finished Work. He cannot see it but by faith he believes. His faith is well founded because

Calvary is not an abstract theory. It is an intrusion into history, the visitation of God in the species of mankind, created for his glory. Thus Calvary is the bridge of redemption that makes the Christian faith triumph, however weak we are. And then there is the road, the highway of the Cross which the redeemed take to glory. And the Scriptures are there to direct us in this world of many good people, but, let's face it, many charlatans. So that when we step out over the river bank, our foot finds the bridge already there. The Scriptures are unambivalent in directing any reasonable person to the spot on the river bank of history where Jesus became flesh, a human being like you and me. The Scriptures never fail. All kinds of people, from all kinds of situations come to this point on the river bank. Some hesitate; some do not. Some are kept back by others, or by their own sense of low esteem. But all the time, day and night across the earth, people are coming face to face with Calvary, and are stepping out into the darkness. And no one who does so according to the bearings we take from the Scriptures, can go wrong. We 'find our feet,' spiritually speaking. That 'stepping forward' is an act of saving faith.

The prospect before us is exciting. It is not an isolated introverted personal experience where our life is at the centre. Rather we speak of the life of our experience which is shared with the church in trans-history. We say trans-history, because history relates to known earthly physical existence. That contrasts with the spiritual, for the church's pilgrimage was initiated in the elective will of God before the world was. It passes through time and crosses history; it touches the physical, drawing people into it, like a stellar body, like the recent comet visiting the proximity of our galaxy in space. But it moves on, with all who are caught up in the Divine power of Christ's redemptive victory. And then at last there is the consummation in glory.

I ask you to become part of this great moving caravan, this

migration of the new Israel in time, which gives you a portion that shall never be taken away from you, an inheritance with the saints in light. Nothing that you are called to endure, however hard, in this brief span you live in time, can be compared with the glory that awaits you.

The foundation of your belief

The psalm speaks of Jesus. Here you are introduced to Christ. How you are espoused to him will vary. But to all he is the eternal Son, 'all in all' to those who love him. Further, he is the object of the church's devotion, as the church is the object of his eternal love. This psalm brings before us the transactions of God's decree in giving dominion to Christ from sea to sea. Yes, Christ is the heir-apparent to the throne of the world, but a world in which God's kingdom comes. The coronation of the King of kings is the exciting prospect to which believers look forward. For you and me to be part of this *scenario* as guests of heaven makes this brief pilgrimage on earth an exciting prelude of seeking to please our Master and respond in love and self-giving to others, just for his own Name's sake.

Look at Psalm Two and see a sequence which strengthens the believers' faith. We see what God will do. Therefore the psalm is particularly suited for those who feel intimidated by the powers of the world and feel that they are victims of an age when evil has won control from God. Lay hold on these truths.

1. God's Derision

He that sits in the heavens shall laugh:
the Lord shall have them in derision.

verse 4

The powers of the world are specifically stated as those who 'take counsel together against the Lord, and his anointed.' (verse 2.) It appears that there is an innate hostility and active rebellion to the Rule of Christ. His is a peaceable kingdom which potentially alters society and makes autocratic potentates obsolete. Wickedness keeps many in a job. Like it or not, this is a fact of life, as true in the affluent and developed society as in others that might be considered pagan. One of the big moral issues of our times is the question of economic prosperity based on the making and sale of armaments and weapons of death. Whether the intent is legitimate defence, or overt aggression, armies are kept by nations at a great cost. The very fact of having great armaments and maintaining them, creates a need to keep the wheels of industry turning, in order to supply the latest updated equipment to match or outmatch rival nations.

Apart from war weaponry, the whole of industrial innovation is drawn into this. Even apparent blessings like the automobile exact their toll. Is it not enough that the casualty toll on the roads in the Western world has been calculated to be greater than those on the battlefield during the Second World War?

The modern world with all its sophistication much of which is admirable, has also the dark side. Many of the unsolved social problems are philosophically accepted as part of the *status quo*. The state comes to terms with evil. Licentiousness and immorality are so forceful that they are considered as incurable, viz. gambling saloons, body shops, drinking lounges. Society does not dig the roots of social ills out. It merely trims the weeds and actually nurtures them, making them blend in with the good in society. The result is that evil contamination spreads like radioactive dust to affect and infect the lives of people in general.

Until the end of time evil will tempt people to ensnare the vulnerable and destroy people. In Britain a prime minister, Harold MacMillan, legitimised gambling by incorporating it into the national investment plans, with a veiled defence that gambling was not overt like that in the Football Pools. In Canada, the nation proudly advertises its national lotteries as a road to success, a short-cut to quick riches, a direct contradiction of moral values, apart from Christian teaching that work is honourable. In the 1990's the Nova Scotia provincial government went directly against a poll of citizens, the churches, the doctors, the tourist industry, and sanctioned a gambling company from Las Vegas, using the respectable international hotel name of the Sheraton. The province then became dependent upon the gambling income to balance its budget. The grim price exacted from the weak and the vulnerable has been a trail of broken marriages, ruined careers, suicides, social distress, family disintegration and child poverty.

The psalmist asserts this ongoing reality of evil powers, often acting through socially accepted pressure groups who claim constitutional rights. There appears to be a vested interest in keeping people from the spiritual arteries that build moral strength to withstand evil.

Some believers despair as they see the powers of the world carving up the heritage of Christ and destroying it, that is the people whom he died to redeem, little by little in the subtle veiled guise of exercising democracy and asserting human freedom of choice. Faith falters, as wickedness spreads like molten lava over the green pastures of settled Christian communities, where Christ's authority is usurped.

But listen, 'God will hold them in derision.' The perpetrators and participants in this sacrilege will face the consequences. Their time of reckoning will come. 'He who sits on the throne of heaven shall laugh at them.' It's true the wicked have their day, and many, let's face it, are carried away or 'taken in' and brought to ruin or living lives of indulgent egotism, unworthy of all higher aspiration. When people forget their Creator, then they care not for him who recreates, who can take us, weak sinful sinners, and make all things new. The world projects Christ himself as an alternate, one who is now a powerless aspirant to the throne of the world of people and the people of the world, one whose day is over.

But there is something else. The powers of the world are really cowards. They feel comfortable like us all when we have others acting with us. The natural human trait is magnified when people are engaged in evil. The powers who plot against God like to have company. When they are alone as individual rulers, they are not quite so sure of themselves. Thus you find a continual sense of insecurity among those who are hostile to Christ. They have every reason to feel like this. They have denied the Son of God and usurped or taken over his rightful heritage.

As the dawn of the Third Millennium breaks in human history, there are signs of great change among nations. For nearly a century, the world was divided into two camps, superficially autocratic and communist, with Russia and China as pivotal, and on the other hand, democratic and capitalist Western Europe and the Americas. That is the ideological division. There really is no complete contrast when it comes to human nature and motivation expressed in politics. All seek goals through expediency. It is generally agreed that the philosophy of Britain's 18th century prime-minister, Walpole, that 'every man has his price' still is the rule rather than the exception, even if this is not overt. The politician by definition bends principle in favour of expediency. The basic contrast is religious, between society based on belief in God and society based upon terminal human life. Being true to the religious demands that expediency is servant to principle. No one is entitled to draw a territorial line on the map and claim a black-and-white contrast here in the religious sense, any more than in politics. For sixty years since the day of Stalin and Roosevelt at the Yalta Conference, the world looked to summit conferences. It looked as if the whole world hinged on this. A precarious peace of nuclear equilibrium rested on 70,000 inter-continental missiles on either side aimed and primed day and night against the other half of the world.

Now the walls are down, no more summits, since atheist communism proved that generic humanism, however well-meaning, is just not enough. As Christ quoted Moses, '... man cannot live by bread alone, but by every word that proceeds out of the mouth of God.' (Deut.8:3; Matt. 4:4; cf Luke 4:4)

But there is still a precarious peace. People live, and look ahead into the century with an uneasy thoughtfulness, that is, if they stop to think. There is no overt symbol of a big summit to mitigate anxiety. The world is 'up for grabs'. And in the uneasy peace, forces are at work, still undefined, anti-christs seeking to undermine where Christ the Son of God has his rightful authority.

Puppets

The heights of power belong to God, to him who is 'high and lifted up', who looks upon the ever changing rivalries of nations, and laughs. Even to the ordinary observer, the whole scenario of world leaders, jostling for positions, sincerely struggling to assure world peace, has elements of the absurd. Why? Yes, because time and again, principle is bent in favour of expediency. Look at Ireland, or Palestine, Angola, or the Koreas, Eritrea or Kosova at the beginning of the 21st century. The players are like puppets, trying to accommodate forces that are diametrically opposed and that relate to the spiritual. There is a conflict of good against evil, God's sovereignty against the usurpers of his dominion which is his alone and to which all human leaders, presidents and prime ministers are answerable as a basic and non-negotiable principle.

St. Paul put it in terms of obligation for every believer in the corporate struggle of Christ's church on earth:

> *For we wrestle not against flesh and blood,*
> *but against principalities and powers, against*
> *the rulers of the darkness of this world, against*

> *spiritual wickedness in high places.*
> (Ephes. 6:12)

We repeat God is always at the summit. God has been likened in Scripture to the eagle. The eagle is the sovereign of the skies. And God is sovereign over the world that he created. We see the eagle is used in history to signify dominance, *viz.* the Roman Empire, Germany, and the United States of America. The love of power brings nations and empires, confederacies and unions, crashing down--that's history's lesson, where the principle of God's sovereignty is not acknowledged. Watch what happens in a European Union which has diluted its Christian heritage. Watch what happens, as countries like Canada divest themselves of the Christian character, in the name of spineless pluralism. God will hold them in derision. Their day is coming, when their glory will be their shame.

The De-Christianisation of society

God looks past the 'front' of nominal leaders. Traditionally in dictatorships, or absolute monarchies, the 'man at the top' made the decisions, even those of life and death. In our revised international groupings, or cartels of nations, presidents, prime ministers, even kings, are themselves controlled by forces that dictate decisions. These may be economic realities, or more sinister to think of, the active de-Christianisation of society. In subtle ways that reflect guile and clandestine pressures, nations and leaders take courses that are hostile to Christian belief and often clearly erode a Christian nation's historic foundations of Biblical righteousness. God sees the whole population of nations, and he sees through the mask of overt hypocrisy that dresses evil in the guise of good, thus disarming people and allaying the suspicions of those who fear the Lord and are concerned for their historic spiritual heritage. *He searches the hearts, he tries the reins.* (Revelation 2:23) He makes an ongoing computerised analysis of power-bases, groups within society that have hidden agendas, that are clearly against Jesus the Christ, His Beloved Son.

The fact is that **God is always at the summit.** In spite of all summits, He has the last word over the councils and conferences of men. Scripture reaffirms this through the prophets and asserts this abiding truth time and again.

God is like the eagle in his omniscience, in his power, in his will. But He is also like the eagle in his love. Nations and empires lack this. We are used to a world where we hear that almost everything is negotiable when it comes to decisions. But this is not so with God. There are no shameful *quid pro quo* deals with God. As the eagle never breaks its love union with its partner, not even when one dies, so God never breaks his covenant of redemptive love that binds believers to his everlasting kingdom and gives them an inheritance with the saints in light.

The psalm here represents praise to the Almighty. Listen to Moses in his great song as he commends it to all, beyond the borders of local and ethnic nationalism. Can you not feel drawn upwards in spirit as he speaks!

> *' Give ear, O heavens and I will speak, and hear, O earth the words of my mouth. My doctrine shall drop as the rain, my speech shall distil as the dew...Because I will publish the name of the Lord: ascribe ye greatness unto our God. He is the Rock, his work is perfect: for all his ways are judgement: a God of truth and without iniquity, just and right is he...For the Lord's portion is his people; Jacob is the lot of his inheritance...as an eagle stirs up her nest, flutters over her young, spreads abroad her wings, takes them, bears them on her wings: so the Lord alone did lead him, and there was no strange god with him.'* Deuteronomy 32:1-12

It is to this, believers are called and chosen to be a part of, forever. God-power never ceases. God does not, and cannot by his nature, abdicate or divest himself of his omnipotence. Therefore where there are those who usurp his authority, he is bound to respond. When? That is God's prerogative, even when he wills. It surely is the proof of his patience and long-suffering that he has not come in judgment upon the world of wickedness but still pleads with men to repent. Is not that the Biblical interpretation of the atmospheric phenomenon of the rainbow? But he will not chide with man forever. In his time, '**He that sits in the heavens shall laugh: the Lord shall have them in derision.**' If we look to political summits for security and peace, surely this must make us think again. The Bible speaks of men as grasshoppers on the earth, in comparison with the Creator. Listen to Isaiah, in chapter 40, as he makes comparison between the power of nations and the power of God.

> *Behold the nations are as a drop of a bucket, and are counted as the small dust of the balance...All nations before him are as nothing; and they are counted to him as less than nothing, and vanity.*

Believers are linked to the power of God

You, who read this, as those who seek the Lord, or are numbered already as believers, are called to dwell under the shadow of the Almighty. Here your iniquities are pardoned, here you have laid hold upon life eternal. You now have the promissory notes of heaven, even though the writing be blurred by your tears of wonder and of joy that, even unworthy, you are one of his choice people and are elected to be a jewel in the crown of his exalted Son. Now you are a citizen of his kingdom with all the rights and privileges of the household of faith. Now you also have power, power with God and power with men. There is no limit to this power. You also are like the eagle. Your love for God will never fail for he has redeemed you. You will rise again like the eagle from all adversity. You will soar up to the heavens like the eagle, on the wings of faith. But it is the uplifting currents of God's Spirit that enables you to do so. Listen to the prophet Isaiah, as he goes on to finish that immortal chapter,

> *They that wait on the Lord shall renew their strength; they shall mount up with wings **as eagles;** they shall run and not be weary; and they shall walk and not faint.*

We do not become independent of God, even though we get 'on our feet,' spiritually speaking. Dependence upon the ongoing therapy of grace is the hallmark of mature humanity, where lives are part of the covenant of God's love. Then the power is 'switched on'. It never fails. Why not? Because, as Isaiah has put it, *He gives power to the faint, and to them that have no might, he increases strength.*

That is why, if it is God's will, you can cross the deepest river, survive the greatest storms, climb the highest mountain, endure the greatest trials -- because God is your strength and has become the driving force of your new life.

Listen to Isaiah, that wonderful evangelist of the Old Testament, who we believe speaks in Chapter 12 for countless thousands, who recognising their own weakness, find their destiny in seeking God's will,

> *Behold God is my salvation; I will trust and not be afraid: for the Lord Jehovah is my strength and my song; he also is become my salvation.*

I love what follows,

> *Therefore with joy shall ye draw water out of the wells of salvation. And in that day, shall ye say, Praise the Lord...*

When multitudes have this conviction, they collectively praise God in a dynamic assertion of his sovereign power over all potentates and peoples of the earth. But there has to be that sense of his immanence. We can have it personally, but collectively this is a different matter. We cannot prognosticate the unfolding of this; it is all bound up with the will of heaven. God does not prevent a great awakening, but the work of grace must take place first in the waiting of hearts. How many, we cannot tell. But what a glorious experiment it would be, if the church were to take God at his word and prove his promise that *he would open the very windows of heaven and pour out a blessing that there would not be room enough to receive it.* (See Malachi 3)

And God's greatest blessing is to experience his Presence from whom all grace flows.

> *Cry out and shout, thou inhabitant of Israel*
> *for great is the Holy One of Israel in the midst*
> *of thee.*

Isaiah 12:6)

And the 'gathering in' to Christ will be like a harvest season, a field of sheaves, full and heavy, with golden grain, or like a glorious sunny day, a blue sea, packed with thousands and thousands of boats, small and great, old and new, all waiting their turn to come into the harbour, after making their voyage. Then 'he that sits in the heavens' shall hold usurpers in derision. All kings and conquerors, presidents and prime ministers, must 'put off their shoes from off their feet', before the Presence of the Most High and his Son Jesus Christ, the King of kings. All must bow in tribute before the Lord's Christ. Many will, even kings, presidents and prime ministers. After all they are just human and have the same dichotomy of spirit and flesh that all people have, except that they are exposed to the warping and corrupting influence of power. Hear Isaiah in his glorious prophecies as his enlightened eye sees light on the horizon of history with all its darkness and portents of disaster.

> *Arise, Jerusalem, and shine like the sun; the*
> *glory of the Lord is shining upon you!*
>
> *Other nations will be covered by darkness,*
> *But on you the light of the Lord will shine; the*
> *brightness of his presence will be with you.*
>
> *Nations will be drawn to your light, and*
> *kings to the dawning of your new day.*

Isaiah 12: 1-3

You see, great things are possible, where righteousness obtains on earth as individuals and as nations. When the time of Christ's appearing shall come, there will be a glorious day for king and beggar who acknowledge the last and enduring dynasty of Christ

> *who is the blessed and only Potentate, the*
> *King of kings and Lord of lords.,*
>
> *who only has immortality, dwelling in the*
> *light to which no man can approach unto; whom*
> *no man has seen, nor can see: to whom be*
> *honour and power everlasting. Amen.*

Ist Timothy 6:14-16

We are bound to ask, what grounds are there for believing that this is true? We quote God's answer in verse 6

2. God's Decree
I have set my king upon my holy mountain

Apart from allusions to the kings like David which God sanctioned in his permissive will, this decree of God refers to Jesus Christ. Jesus is the king of the greater Israel, and the heir-apparent to the throne of the universe. God's decrees are made in the eternal Godhead, timeless, untouchable. The greatest potentates of man's history are but minute organisms compared to the eternal 'I am'. And God's decrees made in the mystery of the Trinity, before the world as we know it came into being, defy analysis or description. There is only this, faith rests in God's Word, for the past or for the future --local terms of human history. The compulsive intellectual belief has become a compulsive spiritual conviction. This believing with the heart, embraces believing with the mind. There is an assent of the mind. There has to be this premise. *He that comes to God must believe that he is and that he is the rewarder of them that diligently seek him.* (Hebrews 11:6) What great things are there for those who seek the Lord! We are then like flowers which open to the sun as it rises in the morning and shines with its rays upon us. What can match the Sun of Righteousness, sending the sunbeams of light to focus on our hearts. What a way to live, lying down and closing our eyes, with our hearts turned to God, until sleep takes over. And then, in the morning, we wake with our hearts turned to him, fed with thoughts of devotion in our minds as we slept on our pillow. I'm sure you know this experience of the natural sun. You have wakened up facing the sun. Its rays have come through the window and touched your face. You have stirred up and said, 'O, what a wonderful day!'

Think how your soul can rejoice to wake up with the rays of the Sun of Righteousness filling your heart. The soul, heart and mind become filled with grace. The result is that well-being and joy soak up your whole body with relaxation and a feeling of utter peace.

Scripture speaks with many voices but one message

The many voices of Scripture make a composite picture of completeness. Thus the decree of God's sovereign will, is corroborated and amplified in the New Testament as fulfilled in Jesus,

> *And the Word was made flesh and dwelt among us (and we beheld his glory, the glory as of the only begotten of the Father, full of grace*

and truth.)   John1:14

...Wherefore God also has highly exalted him, and given him a name which is above every name.

That at the name of Jesus, every knee should bow, of things in heaven and things in earth;

And that every tongue should confess that Jesus Christ is Lord, to the glory of God the Father.   Philippians 2:9-11

But what has that to do with our faith? Listen, it is because of God's decree to exalt Christ, by which Jesus now sits on the Right Hand of the Father and shall yet reign over all nations of the earth, that our salvation is sure. Because Christ is the ultimate winner, those who are his are also winners. This decree which is spelt out in the Covenant of Grace cannot be broken. All else shall dissolve and vanish away and all the works of man shall perish. But those who are willing parties to this saving contract of redemptive love, through believing faith, receive grace here for every time of need, and then in the *great change,* when the mortal is exchanged for the immortal, we are received into the arms of God and into glory for ever more. Hear the apostle Paul, as he goes on in the same chapter,

Wherefore my beloved, as ye have always obeyed...work out your own salvation with fear and trembling. For it is God which works in you, both to will and to do of his good pleasure..

That ye may be blameless and harmless as the sons of God, without blame, in the midst of a crooked and perverse nation, among whom ye shine as lights in the world.

                    Philippians:2:12-15

3. God's Declaration

The Christian faith based on the two Testaments, is not a secret society. The decree of God in the eternal councils of his will, is made known to the children of men. Listen to the words in verse 7;

> **I will declare the decree: the Lord has said to me, 'Thou art my Son; this day I have begotten thee.**

A declaration is defined as a 'showing forth.' It is a revelation, an exhibition, or an illustration. I like that. It is an illustration. We all read books, newspapers or magazines. When these are just columns of words, we get bored. It all appears drab and uninspiring. But what a difference when we see illustrations! These express the written word visually, but they do something more. The appeal is to all the senses. Children read the story of Grace Darling and the rescue of a shipwrecked crew. Then the whole episode is illustrated by the artist. Even those who cannot read can be inspired by the courage of that young girl, the daughter of the lighthouse-keeper, who, with her father, braved the angry seas in the little rowing boat to save the crew.

See how this puts a different slant upon the words of Scripture. We realise that here is an illustration of God's eternal love, his intention to redeem, to rescue, the fallen, to save to the uttermost. Thus the children of God dwell upon the Word, and look for illustrations. As they seek the Lord, and wait upon him, the Spirit of Heaven opens up the words, three-dimentionally. Before them, they see in their minds, glorious pictures of Christ who died for them. They see him dying on the Cross, rising from the dead, fulfilling his own words to the seven-times married woman of Samaria, 'I am the Resurrection and the life'. Walking on the waters, they see his arm outstretched to save them when they are sinking. It is not all self-centred and self-interest. We are moved by the pictures of multitudes being fed, the eyes of the blind being opened, and the ears of the deaf being unstopped. The heart rejoices, looking at good books and illustrations of Christ's victories in history in the lives of his followers. Who could not be touched with the illustrations of the martyrs who were burned at the stake or thrown to the lions in the sports centres of Rome and Ephesus! What careless soul can avoid second thoughts when pictures flash across the television screen or are seen in a newspaper, with hundreds of people, young and old of every ethnic affinity on earth, 'coming forward' in spiritual concern' during the evangelistic campaigns like those of Billy Graham, in the latter half of the 20th century!

What a wonder, the eternal Son making himself an illustration of the Father's will! God is love, and Christ declared that love that will not let go, and whose power lifts people up to taste here of the heavenly so that the soul that was dead to spiritual things, is now alive, hungering and thirsting for righteousness. At times we all just see the print and are taught in our minds by ethical and moral commandments. But the children of heaven who are born of the Spirit, who are the 'children of adoption,' look for illustrations. The print becomes then three-dimensional. We see scenes from Scripture, animated. They become living illustrations of heaven's redeeming love. The soul feeds on these, the heart is affected. The whole body becomes permeated with the elixir of grace. Exquisite joy flows through our being. We unashamedly become intoxicated with Christ. We may compose ourselves in public to comply with reserve and to conform with convention, but when we get a quiet place, we pour out our heart before the Lord and the therapy of the Spirit brings a new concept of health to our whole being. Such is the effect of graphic pictures or a 'showing forth' of our Saviour in the immediacy of his person and the tangible texture of his humanity. God spoke by his Son. He spoke, but in the medium of a living person, like you and me.

> *God, who at sundry times and in diverse
> manner, spoke in time past unto our fathers, by
> the prophets,*
>
> *Has in these last days, spoken unto us by
> his Son, whom he has appointed heir of all
> things...*
>
> *For unto which of the angels said he at any
> time, 'Thou art my Son, this day have I begotten
> thee?'*
>
> *But unto the Son, he says, 'Thy throne O God
> is for ever and ever: a sceptre of righteousness
> is the sceptre of thy kingdom.'*

(Hebrews 1:1 et seq.)

And we read in the second chapter, how Christ is the manifestation of the Word and how the Spirit enables you and me to see the animated Word as if Christ is first-hand, very close, like 'live' television pictures.

> *But we see Jesus, who was made a little
> lower than the angels for the sufferings of death,
> crowned with glory and honour; that he by the
> grace of God, should taste death for every man.'*

(Hebrews 2: 9)

That's it. Christ's Coming on earth, his sacrificial death to atone for our sins, was a living declaration or illustration of Divine love, a faithful fulfilment of the divine intention. This is the Light of the world shining from heaven to a world of darkness. What glorious things are here for you and me! We can leave the broken cisterns of the world, and lift our faces to the Sun of heaven, and bathe in the sunbeams of his grace. We ask you to close your eyes, and yet see with your heart. For in each one of us, potentially there is a heart of flesh, a warm human inclination to respond positively to the spiritual overtures from heaven. Let go any hardness of heart; let the warmth of the Sun of heaven melt all opposition. Expose pride and all posturing, in humble confession before the eternal Son. For even as the Father spoke in these last days by the Incarnation, the Risen Son speaks of his mission, to do the will of the Father, to bring many sons and daughters to glory. There is no other, angel nor man by which we come to know life eternal and reconciling peace where all our spiritual debts are cancelled and all our sins washed away by the Blood of Cleansing.

Hear the Father saying to the Son,

> *Thou hast loved righteousness and hated iniquity; therefore God, thy God hath anointed Thee with gladness above thy fellows.'*
>
> (Hebrews 1: 8 quoted from Psalm 45: 6-7)
>
> *'I will declare thy name unto my brethren, in the midst of the church I will sing praise unto thee.'*
>
> ....And again, *'Behold I and the children which God hath given me.'*
>
> (Hebrews2:12-13,quoted from Isaiah 8:18)

These are glorious words declared unto us in the vivid colours of Christ's suffering as a human being and as the Lamb of God without spot or blemish. Such an irrefutable declaration of Divine redemptive love makes the heart of the penitent leap for joy. You see how the psalms link heaven to history, and the Council of the Godhead to the coronation of Christ, the King of kings. And there in that synopsis of saving truth, we have confirmation of Psalm 110, where both readings declare the mind of the Father, *Sit on my right hand until I make thine enemies, thy footstool.* (Hebrews 1:13)

Reason for confidence

How can any one remain despondent, whatever gloom

overshadows the events of time! If you are already betrothed to Christ by a union of saving faith, and live your life looking to him each day, then you are marked out already in the Lamb's Book of Life, to sit with the redeemed at his Coronation. Use time here as a preparation for glory; redeem it by spreading the good news, illustrating in your life the love of God that Christ illustrated to you. For Jesus is seen in all the portraits of his life and death as the graphic declaration, the multi-dimentional imagery of human drama in flesh and blood. We see Him, as a holograph, against the background of the very stars and part and parcel of our own humanity, yet always consistent, the sinless one in the midst of all human contradictions.

Listen to John in his first letter to the early church,

*'That which we have seen and heard, **declare** we unto you'* -- the Greek word used is *appagello,* to 'tell it over again'. Different words are used throughout Scripture to denote this cosmic Declaration. All ultimately mean 'to illustrate' that which God has revealed. Christ is then the great illustration of God's decree and history will be consummated in the crowning of the Son. That leads our thoughts to the request of the Son and the promise of the Father to grant him all power in heaven and in earth.

4. Christ's Dominion

The Father gave all choice to the Son,

Ask of me, and I shall give thee the heathen for thine inheritance, and the uttermost parts of the earth, for thy possession.   verse 8

or as the NEB puts it,

Ask, and I will give you all the nations; the whole earth will be yours.

But the power of the heavenly is not the same as the power

of the world. Christ's dominion entails the rule of righteousness where people redeemed by his blood, love the Lord and serve the Lord forever and forever. How, or even when, we cannot say. But the promise is, that day will come. At present there are manifold forms of obstruction by the 'powers of darkness' that suppress the Gospel. When the power of Christ's redeeming love will come upon the multitudes there will be a great awakening. The powers of darkness shall be broken like fallen pottery. There will be no vacuum. When I visited a parishioner, a long-time seasoned Christian, she quoted her mother who wanted the church to be open for worship, come storm or snow. 'When the door of the church is closed on the Sabbath day, the devil can be seen dancing on the doorstep' There is a truth in that. There is no neutrality in spiritual things. Small and great, ruler and citizen, are called to acknowledge Jesus the Christ and his dominion, from sea to sea, and to earth's utmost end.

Already in the elective will of the Father, the souls of multitudes are marked out as the inheritance of Christ. This is inclusive of all peoples. You can see that there is a progressive development of a global network of communication. This contrasts to a past age when human society comprised many communities, totally shut off from one another. The skeptics of two hundred years ago, who ridiculed the possibility of this Divine intention ever being realised on earth would tremble if they were alive today in the 21st century. How dumbfounded an arrogant atheist would be if you or I walked into his classroom and dialled on a Global Positioning Unit--similar to a cellular phone--and ascertained an absent friend's exact position on our planet within five to ten feet accuracy. Furthermore, what would such a skeptic say when you or I would then speak to him on land or sea, using signals bounced off a satellite? It is probable that the planet Mars will be the master satellite for communications within the foreseeable future.

Why! We are on the verge of mighty things where the wisdom of this world will be integrated into the purposes of God, where his decrees will be unfolded in our known habitat, to the utter confounding of his enemies. What possibilities, for all on earth to know the salvation of our Lord! Already on the short-wave, multitudes across the world hear radio broadcasts beaming the Gospel of Jesus Christ, day and night. No acoustic voice is lost. It is a capsule of measurable energy. Add to this the spiritual energy of the Divine intention, and any day, any time, the world we know may hear that suddenly the power structure of the world will give way to the power of heaven.

Then it will be Christ, coming in the regal clothing of a King, but shining as the light of the world in the garments of righteousness and holiness, to claim dominion over all nations and all living peoples.

How can we say this with any conviction? Yes, for the reason of logic which we have just given that any sane rational observer or analyst cannot help acknowledging. But secondly, because we are given the prophetic assertion in the Scriptures, that while all else in this transitory world will dissolve, the Word of God will endure forever. And, speaking specifically of the direct declaration of heaven, we have this fulfilment of God's Word connoted with an era of great happiness for those who own Christ's dominion.

> ... *My (God's) Word shall not return unto me void, but it shall accomplish that which I please, and it shall prosper in the thing whereto I sent it.*
>
> *For ye shall go out with joy, and be led forth with peace: the mountains and the hills shall break forth into singing, and all the trees of the field shall clap their hands.*

Isaiah 55:11-12

The dominion of Christ over all nations, has two implications. First all who seek the Lord, who follow righteousness, all who have faith however weak, share in that dominion, that reign of righteousness. And in being the possession of the Eternal Son, they are warranted to rejoice and claim in the first person, 'He is mine, and I am his' forever and forever. There is a glorious sense of peace that flows into the heirs of God who are joint-heirs also with Christ. Thus all such are covered by every benediction from heaven. They respond by giving the glory to God only, the matchless ascription of glory given to the church by Jude,

> *Now unto him that is able to keep you from falling, and to present you faultless before the presence of his glory, with exceeding joy,*
>
> *To the only wise God, our Saviour, be glory and majesty, dominion and power, both now and ever, Amen*

Jude 1:24-25

The second implication is there in the psalm. That is not to aver that all the world powers will give up willingly, the territory they have usurped. Therefore the dominion of Christ in the conquest of nations, inevitably means the destruction of evil. Thus there is an uncompromising judgment which shall come upon the enemies of Christ..

It is prophesied in verse 9,

Thou shalt break them with a rod of iron; thou shalt dash them in pieces like a potter's vessel.

That is what will happen to those powers that will not submit to Jesus Christ, the King of all kings.

But God is a God of mercy. His mercy is offered to all, whatever their provocations, yes, an unlimited redemption. Therefore those rulers who will, are called to acknowledge Christ as Lord and to exercise government according to his holy law and sovereign will. This submission to Christ is connoted with wisdom, verse 10-12.

Be wise now therefore, O ye kings; be instructed, ye judges of the earth. Serve the Lord with fear, and rejoice with trembling. Kiss ye the Son lest he be angry, and ye perish from the way. Blessed are all they that put their trust in him.

Thus as we begin the Third millennium and wonder what lies ahead before a world of awful weaponry and unstable, unpredictable decaying nuclear generating installations, we commend God's answer to all. For there are real grounds for uncertainty, in a global *scenario* which is like a trampoline as we all become the object of reactive forces ready to be triggered off by one slip of a politician's judgment or one mistake of a technical calculation. In this, one accident negatively affects everyone across the earth to a greater or lesser degree. And any observer cannot help being aware of superstition even among educated people, mistrust, hatred, falsehood, propaganda, crowd exploitation. These ingredients of man's make-up mar the vision of a new day of betterment and happiness. Wishful thinking, legislating the most sublime of laws, proclaiming such as no longer politically correct, eliminating them from vocabulary, such cannot prevent them from coming up again on life's pathways. It all adds up to a picture in which self-interest of power cartels suppresses the potential of mankind from feeding the hungry, clothing the poor and housing the homeless, and living in a world which could be an up-dated version of the Garden of Eden. But there will be a new day with the dominion of Christ and the 'meek shall inherit the earth.'

Even as I write, the dawn breaks on a November day. Over the past hour, all was pitch dark outside. Indeed it was so dark that I thought that possibly the clock had stopped, causing me to get up earlier than my usual time. But now I see a change.

There is a reddish glow on the horizon, south of east. The dawn has broken and the light of a new day will soon dispel completely the darkness of the night.

Even so, Christ is Light and his Word is light. He is the Light of the world and his Word in the decretive power of the Father is the dynamic hope for us all.

Our hearts may fail with apprehension when we look with pessimism at the powers of nations and federations of nations, whose philosophy excludes the foundations of the Christian faith and the moral basis of society consonant with the Scriptures. But faith alters our perspective. God will have the last laugh, and his Son, exalted in the heavens will have the last word. As the hymn puts it, *He will reign where'er the sun, doth his successive journeys run.*

Therefore the church with all the diversity of peoples who share the faith can sing with the voice of praise, the anthems of hallowed song, even the Psalms like psalm number two. We can do so with confidence for these are rehearsals for the coronation of Christ, the King of kings and Lord of lords, whose dominion shall be from sea to sea and whose rule shall be established in righteousness for ever and ever.

> The sure decree I will declare;
> the Lord hath said to me.
> Thou art mine only Son; this day
> I have begotten thee.
>
> Ask of me, and for heritage
> he heathen I'll make thine;
> And for possession, I to thee
> Will give earth's utmost line

Psalm 62

1. Truly, my soul waiteth upon God: from him cometh my salvation.

2. He only is my rock and my salvation; he is my defence; I shall not be greatly moved.

3.How long will ye imagine mischief against a man? Ye shall be slain, all of you: as a bowing wall shall ye be, and as a tottering fence.

5. My soul, wait thou only upon God; for my expectation is in God.

8. Trust in him at all times; ye people pour out your heart before him: God is a refuge for us.

11. God have spoken once; twice have I heard this; that power belongeth unto God.

12. Also unto thee, O Lord, belongeth mercy: for thou renderest to every man according to his work.

Soliloquy of the Soul

It might well be said that the most important activity for life is the thinking that takes place within ourselves. There is a world within our beings where ideas are mulled over, information is sifted through, where values are weighed, where interests of others and those of ourselves are considered. This Psalm surely illustrates this. It opens with an assertion of this man's credo.

Truly my soul waiteth upon God: from him cometh my salvation.

The assertion of the psalmist's faith results from that activity of thinking within himself. But the thinking is not simply mental activity. It represents the result, if you like, of coming to terms with all the often contradictory claims upon each one of us, in the creed we believe in, the values we entertain, the time we use, the outlets on which we spend our energies. The great value of this psalm is that we are presented with a coherent picture of a man or woman who has come to terms with the contradictions of this life. And without question and without apology, the key to that happy result is based upon his faith in God's power and his own commitment to live by

41

God's word. We chose out the psalmist's pertinent affirmations.

God has spoken once; twice have I heard this; that power belongs to God. (verse 11)

Then he turns in prayer to God as something natural, something he is used to as a habitual way of life, signifying his communion with God.

Also unto you, O Lord, belongs mercy: for you render to every man according to his work. (verse 12)

And then he illustrates the thinking going on within himself, nothing different from what we all do when we are not listening to others or given over to idleness, watching life by sitting on the fence while others play ball on the field. Is that not what watching games and watching others engaged in human endeavour is, standing on the side-lines of life, uncommitted and extracted from involvement. God calls us all to be players, not onlookers on the playing fields of this life.

The Trinity within ourselves

The thinking has that extra connotation of talking within ourselves. Hear the psalmist speaking to himself,

My soul wait thou only upon God; for my expectation is from him. (verse 5)

What a strange mixture we are! Even within ourselves there are different persons within our supposed oneness. It is not that any single part has a separate existence, but each part seems to have a positive sphere of influence which can make it the dominant factor in our life.

We speak of the divisions which are not determined by any pretentious Freudian analysis nor that made in a psychiatrist's chair, however helpful those might be for remedial therapy. We speak in laymen's terms of every day, apart from those that are purely physical.

The mind

The first division is the mind. It doesn't appear right to talk of the mind as the mechanism of reason. It can be and it may not be . It more often than not is the tool of the irrational. It is a mistake to assume that the mind in the sequences of its potential logic must thereby produce the correct antidotes for human ills.

The mind is not autonomous

You see how one person using his mind reaches one conclusion. Another using his mind plus other different factors in his inner being comes to another conclusion. The mind is a primary part of our inner being. It is the agent of thought. Through its receptiveness and processing of the message of revealed religion, the good news of God's love and forgiveness, whosoever will no longer sees life as a problem but as a solution, not as implying a question but providing an answer. It is not independent but the function of the mind is intricately related to our inner life and by the activity of thinking, can make or break us. We make sense of this world with all its woes, by accepting man as he is, not as a piece of machinery, but in the stark contrasts of his capabilities and the diverse range of his behaviour patterns. These suggest that even the most objectively erudite person often does not 'know himself', as ultimately he must be known by God.

In the dimension of the Jesus people there is a process of change. It is true, sin is in the picture. But then there is the antidote, that puts sin in remission, namely Jesus, the Jesus of Scripture, the Jesus of Calvary, the Jesus of history, the Jesus who is the son of God. And the remission is given 'to as many as receive him'. What a break, when you think of it with the mind, for all those who come up against a stone wall, a cul-de-sac of trapped thinking, which is trimmed to the prevailing winds of the socially and politically and philosophically correct. Now a load is taken of the mind, freed from sin. Christ puts a new song in the heart. We are now care-free.

The mind itself is complex. How concerned we ought to be that it is not deceived. There are limitless possibilities to the mind's activities when it is linked like a computer to the screen of the imagination. The imagination triggers off the mind so that the latter can be subservient to the imagination. Look out when the latter gets out of control, or runs away with you.

The heart

The heart is not an entity in itself, but is really the centre of our being and the location of our affections and emotions. We know that it is vulnerable. It can be taken over. If we regard it as the area of sensitivities of the inner person, then it can be conceived of as big or small. This will determine very much what kind of person we will be and the impact our life will have upon our generation. If the heart is regarded as small and cold and closed up, immune to outside stimulii of human need, unaffected by intellectual thought, basic feelings of egotistic preference or physical passion can become decisive factors.

But on the other hand, if the heart is big, wide open, a network of sensitivities which relax outwards, laterally to our fellows and vertically in spirit to noble aspiration, then you can see that there is boundless possibility for a new consciousness, yes of pain for the suffering of others, but also of promise from the dynamic spiritual resources of God.

Now it is like a great receiving system linked to all the avenues of reception with the sensory antennae of hearing and seeing and all the other undefined modes of awareness, often inarticulate in defintion, but powerfully real in the desperate needs of others, crying silently outwards for 'the touch of a human hand'. Thus when speaking of whole persons, we describe them as 'big-hearted', 'soft-hearted', 'good-hearted'. It is true, with this, a person can be exploited, taken in by charlatans. Therefore there must be a selection even of the compassion that we feel, because this person is sensitive to the whole range of man's sorrows.

The soul

But apart from the mind and heart there is the soul. Now the soul is the very life of you and me. Apart from academic diefinition we can think of it as the essence of the individual, connoted with the mind in its consciousness and as resident within the heart, subject to the emotions of the latter. It has a kind of personality of its own within the individual. It has a vital role within our beings. If its very existence and affinity with the spiritual communion with its Maker is denied or suppressed, then we act and live as if we are crippled, incomplete members of community.

The spiritual is analogous to the physical. For example we can sometimes pinch ourselves with a pin and there is no pain. The flesh for one reason or another is numb. We may be very cold. We may be so absorbed in some activity that we forget about physical pain. Now if we think of the metaphysical or non-physical division, there can be the same lack of sensitivity or reactive response by the soul, the spiritual entity which comprises the very nature of our being, to the thoughts that we entertain in our minds or the feelings from our heart.

This soul is an elusive entity. Some deny it exists. Others try and hide it with every kind of expedient. Some keep it locked up. Some drown out any cries of uneasiness from it by turning the sounds of the world louder. That is why music, the exquisite medium and concomitant of human empathy, is corrupted to hypnotise millions especially of young people, and trap them in sensuality before they awaken to good spirituality. In the dimension of the Jesus people, the soul is no longer numb. It is no longer asleep. It is no longer locked up. It is no longer denied. Touch it by feeling from the heart or by thought from the mind and it responds. It reacts. It has become vibrant and animated. It always retains a persona of its own.

There are great possibilities latent in every one of us. Some confirm our identity with our fellow human beings; others when explored and developed can project powerful individual dynamics, reflecting our own special identity, and can potentially make us great contributors to our community and our generation. You see what happens to the Jesus people -- all Christians are Jesus people, or God's people. Their soul is awakened. This changes the whole picture of our life. The dimension of the Jesus people brings accord in place of discord, harmony instead of agitation, agreement within the individual in place of contradiction, happiness in its most sublime conception, when the word of God is read and heard. Why is this so?

The end of gambling with our destiny

There is relief on the part of those who trust in God as their refuge. They have stopped all exploring of narrow speculative views of life. They are like people looking for an ideal house. One day they fall in love with a house. It seems quite different from what they imagined they wanted. But they fall in love with it, and they move in. They are overjoyed with it. They just love it. You could find a thousand palaces in Holywood or mansions in England, but all these prestigious stately buildings mean nothing. Indeed they would be a liability even to the rich, and their space and emptiness would only accentuate a person's loneliness and unfulfilment. You see, we are not designed to live in palaces. 'Uneasy rests the head that wears the crown'. Christ followers are servants of the king. They are messengers to do his will. Here they are on the move, doing his bidding. Here their needs are simple. For they are humble citizens of Christ's kingdom. They do not need the glitter and glamour of the world. For they are not of the world.

Synthesis of mind, heart and soul means radical change

There are two senses in which their life is radically changed. In one there is the basic spiritual awakening, by which they are born again of the spirit, quickened by the Spirit of God, seeking them out in his elective and dynamic will. In the other sense they live in the world, but the latter is the womb, where the soul is incubated. Life is there within them, vital throbbing, demanding, in all the sacredness we associate or should morally associate with the unborn child in the mother's womb. Because the soul is alive, it's life pervades the mind and heart. And dictates through the spiritual compulsion of the will as the executive of our spiritual nature, the direction of physical energies.

St. Paul calls it the *inner man* in contrast to the physical. Whatever happens in the providence of God, no believer is lost. And it is God's will and the believer's will that the inner man or inner life grow every day in grace and the knowledge of Christ. This becomes a great consolation unique to Christians, as the mortal life ages and decays.

> *For which cause we faint not; but though our*
> *outward man perish, yet the inward man is renewed*
> *day by day.*   (2 Corinthians 4: 16)

This is the spiritual life of the believer. He is nourished by the context of the means of grace, the church, his own religious devotions, his responsiveness to the human and social obligation, his degree of service and selflessness, the commitment to the practical challenges of sharing the building of a community of God's people.

47

From darkness to light

And all this is integrated in the computer room of our thinking. Now there is decisiveness. Now there is guidance. Now there is a man or woman, who has thrown off all the heavy burdens of working out all the problems of the world, and who has cast them all on God and sees Christ as the world's solution. This means literally a load is off the mind. The soul is set free; the heart is full of new and exquisite joy. For the whole life, mind heart and soul are flooded with light, that shines through the door now opened by the will. What light! What a glorious light shines into the heart of those who seek the Lord and open the door to Christ! This is the light that shone upon those who sat in darkness and the shadow of death, spoken of by the prophet Isaiah and fulfilled in the coming of Christ.

> *The people that walked in darkness have seen a*
> *great light: they that dwell in the land of the shadow*
> *of death, upon them hath the light shined.*
>
> (Isaiah 9 : 2)

And Matthew records that this Messianic prophecy was fulfilled with the coming of Jesus Christ, expressed in the consciousness of his mission as Saviour of the world (See Matthew's Gospel, chapter 4:14-16)

The apostle Paul, who himself was blinded by that spiritual light on the Damascus Road, speaks of this light emanating from heaven as saving knowledge. While conscious of the most privileged Christians being still earthen vessels until the end of their earthly pilgrimage, Paul says.

> *For God, who commanded the light to shine out of*
> *darkness, hath shined in our hearts, to give the light*
> *of the knowledge of the glory of God in the face of*
> *Jesus Christ.*   (2 Corinthians 4: 6)

As we analyse the experience of a believer, we see this enlightenment is not just some gnostic exclusive insight of man.

Rather is this enlightenment given to the humble of this world, whose heart-door is open so that the light of Christ shines into them, with its glorious joys. It is the stirring of the soul that makes the will open the door. It has heard the imperatives of the law and overtures of grace. I can see the soul, breaking out of the inner room of its slumber; I can see it rising up and calling to the will, 'Open the door. Let Christ in with all his fulness. Let me bathe in his light. Let His Spirit shine so that I can appropriate all these blessings I see projected on my mind. I hunger and thirst for Him, the Light of the world. I have been brought out of darkness and will never rest again except in his light.'

Hear Paul the apostle, exhorting the people of Ephesus with these words. *'For ye were sometimes darkness, but now are ye light in the Lord: walk as children of light:* (Ephes.5:8) And Paul connotes this light with the spiritual awakening of the soul associated with Isaiah's prophecy chapter 60:1.

Wherefore he saith, Awake thou that sleepest, and
arise from the dead, and Christ shall give thee light.

(Ephesians 5: 14)

Rationalization

Now there is a simplification of life. The inner chamber of our being is peaceful. There is no tortured and contradictory activity, no uneasy accommodation through selective data to keep a conscience from being alarmed. You see the conscience is linked necessarily to spiritual awareness of good and evil. Now there is harmony between the thoughts of the mind, the express desires of the soul seeking the Lord and all the sanctified feelings of the heart. Let us keep this idea of the three persons in one. After all we are created in the image of God. But we have to watch out when we think of the mind as a beautiful intricate piece of nervous machinery. It is indeed that, like the finest computer, one of the wonders of the world. But even as it is capable of being the kaleidoscope of glory in all the exquisite pictures of truth, beauty, righteousness, so also the mind as we well know, can be a horrorscope of infamy, where imagination turns it into a monster of evil.

Scripture now speaks with a dynamic effect

As we read the Scriptures, there is now a language that corresponds to the metaphysical anatomy of man. It is not that Scripture has changed but **we have changed**. It does not really matter what translation we use. For all translations there is a pertinent language which corresponds to the different parts of our life and the functions or the impulses which emmanate from them.

God's Redeeming Word like light

When we think of the spiritual light from heaven, often that light cannot be seen at all. But then that is no problem for any thinking person as we enter the third millenium. We are familiar with forces being powerful yet being invisible. Laser light cannot be seen with the naked eye. Yet it can be used to remove a cateract from a human eye or comprise the definitive mechanism of a missile guidance system. Unseen ultra-violet light from the sun can have serious effects upon our human skin. These are known by their function. Such light is not seen, yet is powerful. God's Word in the Scriptures has that unseen effectual quality, where it convicts and converts, where it is mighty. Who can know the mystery of the workings of the Spirit! But it is true again and again that one person is unaffected by the reading and proclamation of the Word and another in the same gathering is pierced to the quick, to rise to newness of life through the awakening of the soul and receiving Christ, the light.

> *For the word of God is quick, and powerful,*
> *and sharper than any two-edged sword,*
> *piercing even to the dividing asunder of soul*

and spirit, and of the joints and marrow, and
is a discerner of the thoughts and intents of the
heart. (Hebrews 4: 12)

Known in its effects

The language of Scripture speaks to the hearer and is known in its beneficial effect. The person who turns to the Lord hears what God the Lord is saying. The psalmist says here. **God has spoken once; twice have I heard this; that power belongs unto God.** (verse 11) This spiritual dynamic cannot be seen, nor expressed in extra words. But the power of heaven is there like light. Thus the soul feeds on what the mind presents to it and the whole heart is full of desire. Grace when it comes into the heart, is like the tide coming in, in all the fulness of heavenly blessings. The promises of God in all the variety of Redeeming love create overwhelming desires in the heart for the heavenly. The Scriptures become meat and drink. Heart and mind and soul feed upon this. Whatever translations or versions of Scripture are published, there will be language which can be understood by the natural man. The Scriptures of the Old and New Testaments are a rich field for students of literature, for academics whose speciality is linguistics. Classical history attracts thousands to study the Bible, and ethnic origins lead the curious to Old Testament records. I recall a teacher colleague giving a lesson of Scripture in a Scottish classroom. I marvelled at his knowledge, and also the disingenuous way in which he taught the class. There was a gread sadness, because he was a professed agnostic. Do you see what this means! You can have a thousand educated teachers who indeed can teach the Holy Scriptures. But when it comes to the unseen message of the Word, they themselves do not know the power thereof. Paul wrote.

Whosoever does not have the Spirit cannot
receive the gifts that come from God's Spirit.

Such a person does not really understand them;
they are nonsense to him, because their value
can be judged only on a spiritual basis.
(2 Corinthians 4:14) NEB

All Scripture can be understood up to a point. There is much in the language that relates to the metaphysical and moral nature of man and his relation to his Creator. So that a stranger to God's grace may know his Scriptures well. On the other hand you can have someone else who is incapable of much apparent intellectual accomplishment or is even illiterate, who when he hears the Scriptures read or preached, has his mind powerfully affected. Christ has not put any pre-conditions for taking the gift of God home with us from church.

Religious teaching indispensible to education

Religion wisely taught is indispensible for the preparatory education for life, but no system can fill the role of the Spirit or by its excellence displace the primary necessity of grace. And grace is promised to all who ask and seek and knock at the door of the Master. How profoundly yet unseen, the light of the Spirit operates. This is true even in a young person so that grace has broken through the sensory windows of receptiveness. That person now sees spiritually. He sees Christ in all the promises of God's love and in all the provisions of his saving efficacy in his finished work. He runs to Christ like a child to its mother, and clings to him as the *Word made flesh*, clothed in humanity, yet sinless and pure and mighty in his victory, and glorious as he sits on the throne of heaven at the right hand of the Father. Who can speak of these things, the exquisite images that are brought to the soul through the mind, as light floods the heart! Paul tells us in Chapter two of 1st Corinthians, that *eye hath not seen nor ear heard* the things that are revealed to the child of God. They are revealed by the

Spirit. And this coincided with spiritual cognition, by which we become aware or conscious of the spiritual. This should never be connoted with any form of subliminal communication used by the world for the world and manipulation of people.

The superiority of spiritual discernment

There is a simplicity in spiritual things which is often despised and contrasted to erudition. But in the last resort, even the greatest mind will disintegrate and cease to function so that the giant of the intellectual world can lose all coherence and capacity of intellectual knowledge. But whatever happens to the child of God, the simple faith of trusting in the love of God in Christ is the key to a glorious life of immortality. Give me this discernment and let all else decay like this earthen vessel, however wonderful it is as the handiwork of God for this mortal life. For to be spiritually minded is life and peace. (Romans 8:12) In this spiritually enlightened perception, the three components of the inner self are co-ordinated together, mind, soul and heart. As all three are diffused with grace the experience, embracing the eclectic **seeing** of the soul, the **thinking** of the mind and the **feeling** of the heart, is sanctified. Thus the inner man becomes the temple of the indwelling Spirit of God, bringing all the merits of Christ in the overflowing benefits of his redemptive victory to the humble and the contrite. When desires for Christ and all virtue in him fill our being, there is room for little else. It is not that everything in life is polarised into black and white. Not a bit. We take Christ into every sphere and activity, and what Christ stands for become the normative influence.

The effects of dynamic grace

By all this dynamic change we see that prayer and meditation become meaningful, as we read Scripture or share in the exposition of it in worship. If we grasp this basic synthesis of mind heart and soul in their co-ordinated functions, then what we know confirms our faith and what we do not know humbles us.

Consider the mind again. God made clear that while the potential of reason associated with the mind, is a common factor between Himself and man, as we think of ourselves being created in his image, yet His thoughts are quite different from ours.

For as the heavens are higher than the earth ... so are my thoughts than your thoughts. (Isaiah 55: 9) The mind as an entity or faculty and what it thinks can be very different. The contention of Scripture is that in the process of thinking in a sinful world, the mind itself is changed. It no longer sees or thinks logically or reasonably. The injunction of Scripture to make a spiritual turnabout is connoted with a changing of the mind, the *metanoia* of the Greek New Testament, which is inextricably linked to the call to repentance in the Old Testament, viz Isaiah. *Let the wicked forsake his way and the unrighteous man his thoughts.* (Isaiah 55: 8)

Overlapping of function

Solomon wrote of man. *As he thinketh in his heart, so is he.* (Proverbs 23:7) You can see that the relationship of mind heart and soul to one another suggests overlapping. But of course that is reasonable, for any analysis of you or me is purely technical. In reality, we are units, in a wonderful synthesis of faculties. In this we can easily understand that each component part can and does affect the whole. This is so real in the context of a sinful world, that there is **distortion.** The mind then does not reason or thinks rationally. The heart then cannot feel in a healthy way as it should. You could say that it is **infected** by the troubled mind. And the soul which ought to aspire to the heights of communion with God, cannot reach upwards in aspiration, but is a deadweight. It is turned inward in a poisonous inversion of the man's own generic ideas of self- assertion and self-fulfilment.

But let us turn to the positive. Mind, heart and soul acquiesce that Christ is all in all and in this unanimity glorious things follow. We should remember this when we read the devotional writings of Scripture. It means that we will find cross-references of function. We have sought to clarify any confusion. Mind, heart or soul can be synonymous with the whole, simply because there is no contradiction when all three are permeated and sanctified by the Spirit of God. Hear the apostle Paul: *For with the heart man believeth unto righteousness.* (Romans 10: 10)

The great Commandments, in relation to God and our fellow men, define Love as the co-ordination or harmony of all factors in our metaphysical nature. *Thou shalt love the Lord thy God with all thy heart and with all thy soul and with all thy mind.* (Matthew 22: 35)

The different aspects of prayer

In the specific psalm presented to us here, we see this division of our metaphysical anatomy. We are used to thinking of prayer or spiritual communication as direct supplication to God. In fact prayer is a broad term, which may be the **soliloquy of the soul** as we have it here in Psalm 62, or it can be a **whisper**, in the context of a humbling acceptance of rebuke from our God. *They poured out a prayer, when thy chastening was upon them.* (Isaiah 26 : 16)

Prayer is often a **meditation,** as in Psalm 64, where the heart is opened to God and the soul reflects upon his desires. Prayer can in turn be **praise**, **supplication,** pleading or **intercession** for someone else, and it can even be **wishing.**

This last view of prayer in an effectual spiritual sense cannot be separated from desire. We are told that *the prayer of faith shall save the sick* (James 5:15) The word used is used only here, the Greek word related to *eucharist*, the giving of thanks. But the word itself is essentially a **wish** or **desire.** If you picture the hearts of people gathered together before the elders from the church, in the name of the Lord, all full of desire for the healing of the sick, you could say that great things could happen. It is as if the stage is set for mighty signs and wonders. There is no limit set by God for great and glorious things to be seen, even the healing of the body and the mind whatever is wrong. But the glory must be to God. The wishes in the hearts must be sanctified so that the desire itself is dynamically charged by grace. Remember the words of Jesus that speak of the exciting potential of believing prayer.

> *Again I say unto you, That if two of you shall agree*
> *on earth as touching anything that they shall ask, it*
> *shall be done for them of my Father which is in*
> *heaven.*　　　　　　　　　　　　　(Matthew 18: 19)

A **believer speaking to himself**

Psalm 62 is just that. David writes down this soliloquy. It is encouraging for us all, for it is a profession of faith. We see in it phrases of trust in God, evocations of confidence, making the psalm a convincing personal testimony. Prayer is not always directly made to God. Here it is an activity, a conversation between the mind the heart and the soul, the trinity we spoke about. When you get this spiritual exercise, animated by grace, the soliloquy or *talking within oneself,* is not something bizarre or a sign of weak-mindedness. Rather here is a healthy indulgence of spiritual experience. Most of us do this when ever we reflect upon life. It is to be desired and is connoted with thoughtfulness. It is closely linked to personal spiritual development. For we are not called to be unthinking followers, externally motivated by the prevailing climate of opinion even of religion, nor indeed as mindless products of environmental chance.

Two beneficial effects

There are two benefits that come to mind from this spiritual activity, this form of prayer in which we talk to ourselves. First God hears. There is nothing surer than this. He knows everyone of us; especially he tracks the believer's path. *For the Lord knoweth the way of the righteous.* (Psalm1:6) And even when we are not speaking directly to him, he overhears us. In a way God eavesdrops. But I don't mind. Do you mind? I've never heard of a Christian who objected to God overhearing him, in all the thoughts of his heart. I suppose God sometimes smiles when he hears some of the thoughts expressed by some of his most faithful disciples. The great thing is that he hears us at all times. If we are doing wrong, then God can correct us. But here we are thinking of the sublime soliloquy where nothing mars the harmony that exists in the believer. No unforgiven sin spoils the serenity and peace of the trinity of mind, heart and soul. The second benefit is that this is the best therapy in the world. This is a sign of a fully integrated personality. There is no discord, but harmony and unity within the individual.

A balanced development of the human being

In the Christian answer to the restless unease of a sinful world, God speaks, sometimes through the mind, sometimes through the emotions, sometimes but occasionally in a traumatic spontaneous spiritual encounter. In the latter, it is probable that the conversion is really a climax to a long resistance of mind and heart, which at last is broken down in a moment of total capitulation. As if God had been seeking and calling your name or mine. We resisted for a long time. Then irresistible grace breaks down all opposition. Christ comes in, sweeping all else out, and brings a feast for the soul. The mind is filled too, and the heart is overflowing with exquisite desires. And they are not self-centred. They embrace all kinds of people whom we want to share in our new found joy. Isn't that what happened to the Pharisee, Saul of Tarsus, who became a new man, Paul the messenger of Christ to the Gentile world!

God speaks through the mind

When God confronts us with the message of his redeeming love, it often is directly to our minds. The mind then becomes the initiatory factor, the door if you like by which the word of God enters into our inner being. It survived all the objections, or should we say, overcame them. Then it passed through the heart and in spite of many contrary desires, moved on until it confronted the soul. The soul is quickened, or awakened by the compulsive animating power of the word of life.

God speaks sometimes using our emotions

The sensitivities of our heart can be a door or an entrance into our inner being. We are touched by the tragedy of a fellow human being or we are affected by the pleadings of some one broken down on the roadside of life, and there are many like this. The heart then becomes a decisive influence upon the mind. Do not despise the emotions. Where our nature has spontaneity of affection and sensitivity of compassion -- there are many people who are like this who seem to be by nature, the children of grace--God uses this avenue of our emotions. Then the mind is drawn into this experience, where the affections react positively to God, or supreme love as it is revealed in the face of Jesus Christ, and indeed in the face of a suffering humanity. Is not Christ representative of suffering humanity, despised and tortured, rejected, condemned, broken, the man of sorrows? What thoughts charged with emotion come to us when we remember with the prophet, that all this came upon the Son of God for our sakes, when he took our place!

*But he was wounded for our transgressions, he was
bruised for our iniquities: the chastisement of our
peace was upon him; and with his stripes we are*

healed.   (Isaiah 53: 5)

You see what happens. The mind is now affected by the coherent reasoning of the word of God. The soul just cannot sleep in this situation. Dynamic change has come to the heart and powerful images are portrayed on the screen of the mind. The heart and the mind are up and doing; they are under the influence of a greater emotion, even the love, the **elective love of God,** that seeks out the lost, the guilty, the fallen, the deluded, the lonely, the restless, the unsatisfied, the frightened, the confused. You see, the soul becomes affected. There is something going on; it cannot stay in bed in that inner chamber where the curtains were drawn and it was in effect a prisoner.

The spiritual change

How can I tell you in words, the glory of the things that now happen? The soul rises up and takes over in the heart and mind. It demands a re-run again and again of the Promises of God written in the gold handwriting of the Spirit, as they are given in the Scriptures and now made the very structure of our thinking. Now this person sees Christ in all his efficacy and knows then that all the wounds were for his sake, all the suffering was for his sins. But he sees Christ risen on the right hand of the glory of the Father. He sees all this as infinite love poured out on the Cross as a fact of history. He feels the power of heaven drawing him to embrace with all his heart and all his mind, the terms of the new covenant of grace where the mandatory commitment is unreservedly the challenge of living by the Law of Christ.

Direct affinity with God

The soul now has a direct affinity with God, which brings a new dynamic to the life of the man or woman and a new vitality and strength which they never had before. Why? Yes, because the way of the Cross needs more than strength of mind or strength of heart. There must be no sleeping partner. It is the role of the soul to draw strength from God. It is the soul that ultimately has that perpetual affinity which makes it the very definition of life, and validates the claim of faith to life eternal.

But we must go on. Here is a soliloquy. It is preserved by David because he wrote it down and incorporated it into the devotional liturgy for the church. It is to be emulated, something not to be used superficially as a veneer of religion, but personally with sincerity.

A time for being with oneself

This reflects the necessity for us all that there is a time to come apart, to leave the familiar company, even the pleasant fellowship, and set apart a time for **being with oneself.** That is quite simple. The three departmentmental heads of our nature need this. Each has something to say. There has to be this consultation, all in the context of the pervasive influence of the Spirit of God. It is necesary for this review, this interchange within ourselves, of thinking, desiring, and trusting, so that adjustments can be made to bring unanimity . In this way there are no qualifications when we speak of Christ or speak to Christ. And our course is confirmed like that of a ship that has made adjustment for leeway and currents that tend to put it off course and also for deviation, that error that creeps into the compass reading through movement of anything ferrous within the ship.

The use of conscience

The mind can never be at peace without the soul being awake. The heart can never be joyful without Christ filling it with the fragrance of heaven. We do not see integrated people without the soul being the active partner and dominant influence. The soul uses awareness or alertness, to danger, weakness, truth, error, pride, personal limitation as a self-monitoring device. This has to be switched on. If not there can be disaster. It is like the thermostat in the heating system which keeps the furnace from overheating the house.

Or you could think of it as the white walking stick that a blind person uses as he walks along the city street. It is amazing to see how deftly he uses it to feel the kerb of the pavement, to avoid running into lamp-posts or knocking into other people, checking the contour of a shop doorway. Such a function is based on a vast store of knowledge which he keeps fresh and up-to-date of all information relating to his environment, and also his selective requirements.

It would be nice to think that we could leave this monitor on automatic. Alas we grieve because this leads to disaster and we have known the bitterness of this. This monitor which is used by the soul is **conscience.** One thing we should remember is this, that the conscience can be very tender and vulnerable to false alarms. We should never accept knowledge of a mandatory spiritual or moral nature uncritically, and certainly not as authoritative which is not consonant with God and his Word. Many good intentioned people have been led astray by entertaining knowledge or science, (these are interchangeable) based on the dictates of group persuasion, sincerely held, but not generically a matter of conscience. Conscience is a universal monitor. Any knowledge projected as obligatory which is not objectively a universal principle imprisons the soul in parochial bondage. Rejoice the Lord is king, our Lord the Christ who sets the prisoner free of every narrow insular interpretation however much it is the sacred cow of tradition. Our conscience is answerable to God for ourselves.

Considering the conscience of other people

But we are answerable to God for the conscience of others who may be weak. Sometimes through narrow insular teaching, or personality disposition, they make conscience of localised cultural or religious tradition or denominational identity. Fear then makes them act or constrains them from enjoying the full liberty of the children of God which Christ won for the church to free it from prejudice or any kind of man-made bondage. Yet many are good people who simply have a weak faith. It is like a fire alarm in your home. If it is set too high, it will go off, if the house gets warmed by the sun on a summer day, or if the Sunday dinner is cooking in the oven in the kitchen. You know that there is something wrong there. Now you can adjust the fire alarm, but alas it is very difficult if not impossible to adjust a tender conscience that has been set by unbalanced teaching or is influenced by misinformation. Do we laugh at such people with their weak conscience? We dare not. No, we are to consider them, so that they are not offended in what we do or not do. The question of conscience relates to the relationship each one of us has to God, that is, the morality of our actions in their impact upon others. If this is a negative impact in weakening a faith or confirming a prejudice, then we have a problem before God.

The solution is not straightforward. Bold assertion of liberty may emancipate one person from prejudice. On the other hand, it may offend the conscience of someone else, so that confusion and distress may further weaken his faith and bring disruption to his Christian life, or even destroy his faith. Paul puts it like this...*when ye sin so against the brethren, and wound their weak conscience, ye sin against Christ.* (1st Corinthians 8: 12) That aberration of conscience is sin. Clearly we are to exercise wisdom and discernment in the knowledge that we accept. And because we seek to follow Christ in the spirit of brotherly love, we will consider the conscience of others, so that they are not offended in what we do or not do. That is not easy, for sometimes we should as Paul suggests in his rebuke to Peter, not capitulate to insular traditional prejudice, but boldly give leadership even at the cost of being maligned. (see Galations 2:14) Let us test the knowledge we allow into our minds. Hear John who saw the subtlety of false teaching posing as Christianity. His injunction to his hearers then is as relevant as ever as we enter the third millenium since Jesus came on earth.

> *Beloved, believe not every spirit, but try the spirits whether they are of God: because many false prophets are gone out into the world. Hereby know ye the Spirit of God: Every spirit that confesseth that Jesus Christ is come in the flesh is of God:*
>
> *And every spirit that confesseth not that Jesus Christ is come in the flesh is not of God: and this is that spirit of anti-christ, whereof ye have heard that it should come; and even now already is it in the world.* (1st John 4:1-3)

Check it yourself, for there is much in this world that passes for truth which really can bring us mischief and distress. Remember, it is the truth of God's word that sanctifies even religious tradition. And however sacred a tradition may be, for that reason alone it has no justifiable hold on the conscience and may well be a burden rather than a blessing to our Christian life. This is not a licence for us to live our lives with reference to God alone. God's Word which governs our conscience means that our lives relate to the conscience of other people and very good people, though we may differ in many respects from their views. Thus we sin if we wilfully or selfishly offend the conscience of other believers or weaken their faith. A mature vibrant dynamic faith can afford to be benevolent, and make allowance for the good of others who may be sensitive. Paul examines this relation to the conscience of other people in his first letter to the church at Corinth where there were residual elements of idolatry in eating food donated for idols. Look, he says, in effect. just go along with unbelievers, *asking no question for conscience sake* and eat what is put before you. But if it is pointed out by sensitive people that this food is linked to idols, then I advise you not to eat it for you may offend their conscience. (see 1st Corinthians 10:25 - 35) The Christian has great liberty *for the earth is the Lord's and the fulness thereof,* but we abuse that liberty if we offend the conscience of another believer. The guiding principle must be, no one should be looking out for his own interests but for the interests of others. Live in such a way as to cause no trouble either to Jews or Gentiles or to the church of God. NEB (1st Corinthians 10 : 24, 32)

Jesus told the parable of the Sower illustrating that the seed of God's Word must take root in the animated ground of our whole being. Thus the message of the Word must reach into the ground of the soul. Through this **in-depth** religious interaction, our life style as the approved expression of religion of our peers or community, becomes secondary and relates to wisdom or discretion and personal preference. The affections of the heart will be dominated by a sensitive compassion. This does not mean that we cease to love ourselves. Why should we? We are all precious in God's sight and the very experience of grace gives us an awareness of human worth, our own as well as that of others. Therefore it would not make sense to discount ourselves. When we read the two great commandments which Jesus came to illustrate in his self-giving,(see Matthew 22: 35 - 37), the second is like the first. We are to love others as we love God. This is a command which involves grace because the love we are to show to our neighbour is *agape*, the same kind as that affection with which God has loved us. Thus the love we project is the responsive affection resulting from grace when God first loved us.

We are also to love our neighbour as we love ourselves

But even although the equation of loving our neighbour is

similar in essence to the first commandment of loving God with the whole heart and mind, yet the criterion is given that we are also to love our neighbour **as we love ourselves.** This increases a sense of self-worth and self-esteem, not to be confused with pride or an inflated sense of importance. Do we love ourselves? Of course we should. If not we will love other people less. St. Paul made this clear. *For no man hateth his own flesh.* ((Ephesians 5: 29)

Sacrificial love

The sacrificial love which has made men and women give their lives for Christ and his Cause was never a blind emotion or misdirected action. The calm serenity with which martyrs --see Foxe's book of Christian Martyrs and Alexander Smellie's Men of the Covenant -- went to their death was always an irritation to their killers in the name of the church or the State. The love that takes root in a soul is linked to light, the light of God's Word and to the worth of every man who is created as one of the family of humanity for the glory of God.

When we hear of the suicide bombers of a political Muslim movement blowing up themselves and nineteen Israeli young men on a bus near Tel-a-viv, even as I write, it contradicts the Christian teaching of supreme sacrificial love, that Jesus spoke of and personified, *Greater love hath no man than this, that a man lay down his life for his friends. (*John 15: 13). Christian love is illumined with grace in mind, heart and soul. Therefore anything less is mistaken and evil for it is not consonant with principle in the universal obligation to treat all life as sacred. The love that brought death to the Christians martyrs is a witness to the world, a light that cannot be hid and because it is generically linked to Christ, these martyrs have a place in glory that words can not describe and which angels covet as well as saints.

Reflection a necessary exercise for human health

In Psalm 62, we see that self-reflection comes into it as a very healthy part of the spiritual experience. That self-reflection means, we can talk to ourselves. We can talk to God and we can talk to other people. This makes our religion have a balance as we speak of it having depth. This does not mean that the intellectual ground should be overworked. If that were so, one strikes the subsoil, which rejects good seed. We must have seen this where parents with great zeal have grilled their offspring with too much catechism and creed, so much so that the children have grown up, only to abhor religion and turn their back on their heritage. You see, *in-depth* must mean *in mind heart and soul.* On the other hand let *in-depth* correlate with over-much play upon the emotional side, and there can be as a result an imbalance, where the intelligence is bypassed and undue emphasis is placed on the *experience of the moment.*

With reference to the parable of the Sower told by Jesus, the secret is to let the deep soil of the soul come up or be dug up. Let there be a complete turnover of the soil of the inner man, just as the soil is turned over by the plough in order to sow the new seed. The result will be that the spiritual or that which is concerned primarily with the soul, becomes dominant. It is brought up to the forefront of our lives. But it is animated, dynamic. It is alive. And from it the roots go down into the heart and mind. The effect will be that the fruits of that life will now be spiritual and the spiritual will be from the good seed of the Word. No one wants to be digging up roots but to take and to taste of the fruits. Never was this more true of the Christian. We grow *being rooted and grounded in love* (Ephesians 3: 17) Let the mind absorb and enjoy the great doctrines of the faith and debate all the different shades of interpretation, held by believers through the ages. That is, if the person has nothing else to do. Let him talk about pre-destination or election, pre-millenium or post-millenium, the virgin birth or baptism. They all have their place but our opinions will not change their importance as views consonant with the Word of God. Nor for that matter will all the talking change you or me for the better except perhaps to deflect us from showing the fruits of the spirit in our day and generation. The change that justifies the experience of grace is a dynamic contribution to those who relate to us. For the essential spiritual expression of our faith or the fruits of the Spirit working in us as the proof of our adoption in Christ as the sons and the daughters of God are *love, joy, peace, long-suffering, gentleness, goodness, faith, meekness, temperence.* (Galations 5: 22)

The priority of the spiritual

We see this in Psalm 62 where David talks to himself. What has the soul to do, to become primary? We think of believing or having faith so often as a contrast with good works, as if faith is something hidden in the background. But that is not so. James, the apostle, pointed out that faith and works should go together. So that faith, because it is a *fruit of the Spirit,* should co-exist in a witnessing expression among all the other fruits of love, joy, peace, long-suffering, meekness. David shows how primary it is. You see we believe with the heart and confess with the mouth, but both these functions are nullified or are invalid unless the soul lives. This is it, the soul is alive, spiritually alive and it lives by faith, faith in the Son of God.

Faith takes precedence, for by it we are dynamically spiritual. All things are possible because the soul is quickened and lives. This person can never be the same again. All things have become new. Whatever his attainments, great or small, and he should go all out with heart and mind to serve God and his fellow men, nevertheless his soul lives by faith. *The just shall live by faith,* said Habakkuk in the Old Testament and

Paul in the New, (Habakkuk 2:4; Romans 1:17)

What God means to me.

You could say that David puts down in this prayer, **What God means to me.** This is primary; this is the essence of the spiritual. He is illustrating this spiritual content within himself. The three persons are there within him by inference. The soul is there. It is silent before God, **Truly my soul waiteth upon God; from him cometh my salvation.** (verse 1) The soul is uppermost. This is the spiritual, opened up and brought to the surface like ploughed ground . The good seed germinates and grows. Soon it becomes green and rich with crops or fruits. They all need the sun of righteousness to nourish them. Thus the person of the soul, this third person of our nature becomes the dominant factor in dynamic living.

While the heart and mind have correspondence with the humanity of Christ, the soul has this, but something more. It is like an echo from eternity, of the ages in the past before sin broke that communion of the spiritual. But we rejoice that it is also an earnest of the future. Then the mind and heart will cease to have the connotations of our mortal life as we know it now, but the life of the soul which lives here, will then be intensified in the extension beyond death and the liberation from the earthly which that implies. David talks within himself.

> **In God is my salvation and my glory:**
> **the rock of my strength,**
> **and my refuge, is in God.**(verse 7)

Yet all this is due to the fact that priority is given to the soul and therefore to the **spiritual.** The mind becomes the tool of the soul. The soul uses the mind for its spiritual ends, just as it dictates through its spiritual power to the heart and will and dynamically energises the whole life, subordinating all faculties to seeking the glory of God. The mind can not be nearest to God. God's thoughts are very high above our

68

thoughts. All aspiring to knowledge as God knows with the mind is very vain. Was this not the undoing of mankind, when he coveted the knowlege that would make him equal with the Creator? (see Genesis 3: 1 - 7) And like the race to put a man in space, in the 1950's, man under the cloak of altruism, still strives in this contemporary world, where the 'scientist' is worshipped, to find the hidden secret of life itself, coveting the power to control the creation which alone belongs to the Almighty.

Cultivating the fields of the spiritual mind

Thinking good thoughts follows spiritual enlightenment. Salvation is not to be construed as a vague general description of automatic deliverance. There is something amiss if we do not go on thinking constructively and devotionally about the different facets of God's truth and our relationship to them. If we do not think about God and the manner of Christ's love by which we are called and chosen and justified and forgiven; by which we are forgiven, and redeemed;by which we are sanctified and being saved, then it is reasonable to believe that our spiritual life will be undermined. *We should always have a reason for the hope that is in us. (Ist Peter 3:15)* There is something amiss however beautifully cultivated a farmer's field may be, if he leaves other fields adjacent to it uncultivated and neglected. You can see the effect. The weeds that grow freely in the latter will do mischief to the field that is cultivated. Likewise it is not God-honouring to leave the spiritual cultivation of the mind neglected.

Stocking the mind with the promises of God

The mind can also be considered as a storehouse for heavenly thoughts, which the soul can feed upon in dark days when God, it seems, is withdrawn from us. Whether we like it or not this is true in the experience of many believers. Then the soul searches through the cupboards of the mind and lays hold upon promises of God. Some that we thought little of are now valuable and we treasure them. Preachers should use the Word of God freely from the pulpit. When they are uncertain of their own words, they should bring out the promises of God and give them to the congregation.

The soul can be starved of the fuel that gives spiritual health and happiness to the 'whole man'. The effects of this deprivation are chronic. The soul is starved, just like an engine can be starved of fuel and will not function properly. When we starve ourselves of spiritual fuel, we experience loss, low self-esteem, subjective hurt, shame, defeatism impotence despair, to name just some of the negatives.

What happens is that we start drawing upon our capital and of course that eventually runs out and we become spiritually bankrupt. But the great thing about the Gospel is that we can declare our bankruptcy at the feet of Christ. To the degree that we perceive this, this never unresolved disparity between aspiration of the soul to heavenly things, and our earthbound inability to grasp the stars, we face the facts.

Facing facts

When we face the facts of life, we are in effect coming down to earth, in a realistic and reasonable evaluation of our spiritual standing. It is like looking at a chart and identifying our position on it, after being driven off course for days by a storm. Only by accepting that we are somewhere off the course we were sailing -- this is called our assumed position -- is it possible to calculate our true position. We will not know what exactly our true position is until we take the sights of the sun or the stars. But the assumed position is the starting point. If we think of this as an analogy of our spiritual condition, we see it as imperative that we are realistic in facing the disparity between the course of the highest aspiration, which the soul is designed for, even **to glorify God and enjoy him for ever,** and our true position, somewhere off course, pushed there by winds of false doctrine or subtle false signposts, that catch our eye with the ever changing neon lights of successive fashion. Do you see that this is a progressive step in our thinking? We know that we are found wanting. This is why Christ came into the world. This is why we have to get a glimpse of Christ, in all his efficacy as a Redeemer, in all his beauty as the Saviour, in all his power as the magnet of forgiving love, in all the sufficiency of his Unsearchable Riches of grace, provided for sinful men like you and me.

In him our highest aspiration is represented in his incomparable loveliness, sinlessness and righteousness. To know him, to get a sight of him is the knowledge we need to get back on track, the course that is set before us in our life here. This contrasts with the cheap empty existence of lives that try to make do with substitutes, with copies, with replicas, with visual symbols. These ultimately only accentuate the absence of the real thing. How poor the affluent of this world are compared to those who have access to the riches of heaven. And the riches of heaven are provided in the Word of God, the holy Scriptures, in all the variety of God's promises, and all the accuracy of his commandments and his statutes. These become for us the coveted commodities, necessary for getting back on course when we have strayed. Hear David in another psalm:

The law of the Lord is perfect, converting the soul:
the testimony of the Lord is sure, making wise the
simple; the statutes of the Lord are right, rejoicing
he heart; the commandment of the Lord is pure,
enlightening the eyes.   (Psalm 19 : 7 - 8)

You see these are the necessities of life, our spiritual life in this world. These must be on our shopping list. But see what they do for us. The soul is converted, the heart rejoices, the eyes are enlightened, the simple are made wise. This is a sacrifice of prayer acceptable to him. For David his trust is in the one, living and true God, our God too, of Abraham, Isaac and Jacob, the father of our Lord and Saviour Jesus Christ. Upon this God and him only David rests his hope, saying, within himself, **My soul, wait thou upon God**. (verse 5)

The experience of grace affects our whole life

The whole of our being is called to share in the blessings of heaven. What profound effects they have upon our life in this world. But the blessings of heaven require that our heart be affected with desire, like a person who is hungry or thirsty for the living waters that are found in Christ. The mind also must be turned to God to dwell upon him in the holiness of his law and the offer of his grace. God has given us the great structural beams of the revelation of his Word through the prophets and apostles, and Christ being the chief corner stone of all. We are not called to grasp all the wonders of God's word and understand the mysteries of truth. Who can any way? It was to a puzzled educated man Nicodemus, that Jesus addressed the immortal words that describe the essence of the Gospel.

For God so loved the world, that he gave his only
begotten Son, that whosoever believeth in him
should not perish, but have everlasting life.

(John 3: 16)

Here is a new beginning, to believe this! Then as the person waits, what expectation, what excitement, God hearing that another soul is laying hold upon his Word, the powerful Word which shatters illusions about ourselves, punctures pride, then brings hope, forgiveness, reunion with God, reconciliation, peace, joy and dynamic spiritual power. There is no end to the good things for those who wait upon the Lord and wait for the Lord, like the queue who wait for the store to open its doors, offering free gifts. What heavenly gifts that are provided for the penitent. How matchless is the robe that is given to cover the sin of the penitent. When you look and see that it is the righteousness of Christ, woven in the sufferings of the Cross, but stamped with the insignia of the King of kings. Yes, I found like ten thousand others, the words of Christ's victory given to Martha, the sister of the Lazarus. They are written, embroidered on this covering of righteousness of Christ, especially designed for sinners like me. I saw them one night in the darkness when sin and shame brought me very low. Then a light, it came from Christ (John 12:46) shone on the screen of my mind, and my soul grasped it with joy. I rose up and worshipped him whose love is so great and whose forgiveness has such efficacy. These are the words.

> *I am the resurrection, and the life: he that believeth*
> *in me, though he were dead, yet shall he live; And*
> *whosoever liveth, and believeth in me, shall never*
> *die.* (John 11: 25-26)

People like this, all over the world, whose lives are being transformed by heaven's grace are being added to the church daily, as elective love seeks them out to be part of the glory of the new world.

If you were to know the testimony of the redeemed, you would hear that all the promises and declarations of God's love and Christ's accomplishments on their behalf were woven into the embroidered garments of his righteousness. And these are worn by the church as the collective witness of God's people.

Hear the psalmist as he stood back from the pageant of history and saw down the centuries of time, the church coming forth from all its struggles, all its persecutions, all its mockings, all its pain, all its weakness, all its faults, but chosen by the effectual power God's elective will.

> *My heart brings forth a goodly thing;*
> *my words that I indite*

Concern the king: my tongue's a pen
of one that swift doth write.
Behold the daughter of the King
all glorious is within;
And with embroideries of gold
her garments wrought have been
They shall be brought with gladness great,
and mirth on every side,
Into the palace of the king,
and there they shall abide.
   (Scottish Psalter Psalm 45:1,13,15)

When morning breaks on the soul

   What a moment when clouds clear, when the waiting is broken, when the morning is come for our soul. For surely it is all of this and more, with the coming of the Spirit of God to the door of our receptive hearts, now opened from the inside by our will. What matchless joys accompany the visitation of Christ himself, for the Spirit makes him known to us as the express image of the Father. (Hebrews 1:3) Now, the soul runs to embrace him, his redeemer, who loved him. The heart is now full; Christ has come into it. There is no room for anything else. The mind is there with the lists of God's promises, Christ's credentials as God's Son, and the evidences of his sacrificial love. And even as the soul embraces the one who is his Saviour, he feels the dew of heaven fall upon him, and he rejoices. Doubts are gone, all other desires are gone; the fragrance of heaven fills the heart with the intoxicating elixir of the heavenly. Now, grace permeates his inner being. He breathes in the breath of the spirit. The soul lives with dynamic life. The heart is soaked with grace, the emotions are unashamedly expressed in tears so that repentance and faith mingle together in a reciprocal love for Christ. The mind also with all the thoughts of God's Word is saturated, so that the thinking mingles with grace and joy in the Holy Ghost. It is not unusual for the whole experience to affect our physical being, to relax all tension, to permeate it with the therapy of spiritual healing and to diffuse throughout our whole person, a matchless feeling of well-being and joy that lingers with us. *In dwellings of the righteous is heard the melody of joy and health.* (Psalm 118:15)

This experience is not just subjective, an exclusive egotistical transaction between me and God. Of course it is personal, but it is also true that this is shared with others who have the same inclination, the same mind for heavenly things, the same desire to find Christ in all his efficacy, and trusting in Him as the solution for the equation of life's deepest problems, our sins, our guilt, our shame, our foolishness, our emptiness, our hopelessnes, our misery, our fading strength and our finite failure. Why on earth should people wrack their brains, and wear themselves out seeking answers to the human problem by human reason, and all the time, the equations of the universe itself and all the dynamic secrets of our existence, both the chemical and teleological, of our biological make-up are already computed in the mind of the Creator, who presents to man the world over, the solution of his redeeming mercy which is as inexhaustable as the heavens, and all the unfathomable depths of his judgments that make salvation our possession through the merits of the Cross and give us to be heirs of glory.

Living our lives spiritually

You can understand that life is changed for you and me, when we have this transformation of our inner being.We just cannot hide such great things from other people round about us. It is not that all in the garden is rosy from now on. It is a fact of the Christian life that the mind has a record of many doubts, many intellectual fights, many attacks which weakened faith. Also if you examined the heart of believers, you would see the scars of many wounds, deep ones of sorrow as well as the superficial scratch marks of irritation. But the wonder is that all these healed and in retrospect, the believer could tell you that when the heart was broken, Christ himself came to him and according to his promise in his mission of redemption, his love in all its efficacy brought healing.

Listen to the mandate given to the Messiah for Christ to fulfil as the mission of redemptive love in reclaiming the ground of human society, taken over by sin.

The Spirit of the Lord is upon me; because the Lord hath anointed me to preach good tidings unto the meek; he hath sent me to bind up the broken- hearted, to proclaim liberty to the captives, and the opening of the prison to them that are bound ...This day is the scriptures fulfilled in your ears.

(Isaiah 61:1; St. Luke 4:18, 21)

You see the difference for us when we live spiritually! We have a secret weapon for all our conflicts; we have a secret strength for all our weaknesses; because we are on the Lord's side, we are his servants to do his will. It means that our lives are lived in the sunshine of his presence, and even when we are in darkness it is said, if we give out in the name and service of our Master God will be a light unto us. Listen to the glory and grace that are given to us as we work for our Lord's human rescue business.

Then shall thy light break forth as the morning, and thy health shall spring forth speedily: and thy righteousness shall go before thee; the glory of the Lord shall be thy rereward.
And if thou draw out thy soul to the hungry, and satisfy the afflicted soul; then shall thy light rise in obscurity, and thy darkness as the noonday.
And the Lord shall guide thee continually, and satisfy thy soul in drought, and make fat thy bones: and thou shalt be like a watered garden, and like a

spring of water, whose waters fail not.
(Isaiah 58:8,10,11)

The race set before you

All the slings and arrows of fortune may wound, all the contrary winds may push you off course for a while. But remember, you have one who is mighty and who binds up the wounds and injuries of the mind, and whose special work is to bind up the broken heart. And what of you when you are driven off course like a ship! Wait and see. It is not the end. The storm will blow out even though it last many days. And the sun will come out, and for you it will be the Sun of Righteousness. You can take a sight with the sextant of your faith; and if you like, you can check this with your Global Positioning System, and you will get back on course, the course set before you. Know this course; make it your business to know it for you. The race set before you by your Lord will differ according to the diversity of gifts and challenges of service, for different people but there is this common denominator with all the redeemed who journey to Zion through the ages, they will go forward, looking to Jesus. the author and finisher of their faith. (Hebrews 12: 2)

And what of my soul?

The soul talks to God; it communes with God. Sometimes it is silent; sometimes it speaks. Its language is eucharistic, and on earth that praise of God as the soul sees eternal things of the spiritual, is expressed through the heart in love to God and others, and it takes coherent and vivid form in the mind, in dynamic thoughts. Soul heart and mind are one within us. Each one assents as we love the Lord and strength comes to the sinews of our whole being, as the soul leads in praise.

I love the Lord, because my voice
and prayers he did hear

I while I live will call on him
who bowed to me his ear.   (Psalm 116: 1,2)

The thoughts in the mind do not originate there. We assimilate them from the revealed Word of God. Their import takes form and become images within the mind. Language is but a vehicle where the ideas are presented on the screen of the mind. The soul and the heart join in to rejoice in the abundance of spiritual blessing, and adoration of the ineffable love that Christ embodies for us as our Redeemer and Lord. Language is wonderful for with it we can go back to the different junctions of God's truth. There we can load up the mind with the resources for the soul. We can then take them back and store them. Memory is a great faculty. We can use it with all the megabytes of its potential for our spiritual growth and our guidance. It means also that we are at one within ourselves. So that when the soul is stirred up and sees eternal things, sometimes looking at old things but in a new light, the eyes of the understanding being enlightened, then there is a feed-back into the mind. Then the mind gives us graphic views, not of abstract or surrealistic fantacies, but interlocking truths that all seem so reasonable and normal. Why? Yes, because living by faith means that we believe all things are possible with God, and faith appropriates this confidence and acts on God's revealed will for us.

Looking over the shoulder

Do not forget the heart. The heart or the affections, looks over the shoulder of the soul, and the affections which of course let go all other loves, are specially drawn to Christ anew. This experience goes on within us time and again. Nothing can keep the heart back. It wants to share with the soul as the mind is illumined with the vivid projection of the promises of God, all the good things of the heavenly.

The affections have never known such intensity of love. The heart is filled with delight; the emotions cannot be left out of this. The spiritual intoxicates the whole consciousness. The mind is almost overcome as thoughts fill it. You see, words can only express in part. But the view even a glimpse that the soul had, now portrayed on the mind is a feast for the soul. This is a wonder that will never cease, that Christ died for me and rose again for my justification. And the heart cannot get over it It could possibly understand a love loving one who turned to love God, but this is something else. Faith means that hope springs up within us instead of despair. And God honours all the cheques that we use to draw from our account of faith in the bank of grace. God must smile at times when he sees those who serve him, coming to the throne of grace and asking for large amounts. But no one in earth nor in heaven can ever say that God refused him the grace for any time of need and every task in his service. So that the heart is repeatedly moved as we dwell upon this love supreme.

> *Because the love of God is shed abroad in our hearts by the Holy Ghost, which is given to us. For when we were yet without strength, in due time Christ died for the ungodly. For scarcely for a righteousn man will one die; yet peradventure for a good man some would even dare to die. But God commendeth his love toward us, in that while we were yet sinners, Christ died for us.* (Romans 5: 5 - 8)

Talking to other people

We have looked at the soul talking within himself; the believer talking with God. But there is something missing. Haven't you seen that too? If this faith is to be accredited, the believer must also talk to other people. There is a responsibility to explain himself. He cannot live in a sin-darkened world with all the cries of the lost coming to his ears, and all the anguish and pain of those who have fallen into the cracks of a broken and selfish society where the proud and the rich insulate themselves from the common obligation of being our 'brother and sister's keeper' without telling about this gold mine of spiritual happiness that makes the poor and the needy rich for ever more.

It is too bad if we are misunderstood, or mocked, or laughed at. Why, isn't that how people reacted to Noah's preaching, to their loss.(2nd Peter 2:5) On the other hand the people of Nineveh responded positively with repentance to the preaching of Jonah, and they were saved. (Jonah 3:5)

What God means to you and me

This is a note that the psalmist strikes throughout the psalms. What God has done for him, he wants this for other people too. Now he ceases to think of himself and focuses on other people who are as needy as himself.

> **Trust in him at all times; ye people, pour out your heart before him: God is a refuge for us.**
>
> (verse 9)

There is no sense of *us* and *them*. He sees himself as identified with humanity, and he wants people everywhere to drink from the Fountain of Life, in contrast to the broken cisterns of the world. He wants other people to find out for themselves what God can do, and what God can mean to them, to give them peace of mind. For he was pointing to the formula which worked for him and works for all the followers of the way, and expressed so beautifully by the prophet Isaiah,

> *He will keep him in perfect peace whose mind is stayed on Thee.* (Isaiah 26:3).

The word used for the mind by Isaiah is comprehensive. The whole spectrum of a person's thinking, and even dreaming is inferred here. That is none other than our imagination.

Being saved from our imagination

While we think of the mind as part of the infrastructure of our thinking, the mechanism to which we attribute the identity of the intellect, imagination is an elusive intangible entity. Hear the psalmist in the second verse of Psalm 62,

How long will ye imagine mischief against a man?

The imagination is proven to be that uncontrollable element within our make-up. It is so uncontrolled that it will contradict logic and activate pre-emptive violence against others, because it is charged with non-trust, non-faith or suspicion which is a fruit of evil, and a proof of original sin. An illustration of the uncontrollable nature of the imagination was seen during the Iran versus Iraq war in the 1980's. The commander of an American battle cruiser, patrolling in the Persian Gulf was told that radar spotted a plane approaching. There was an immediate alert and suspicion that it might be an attacking fighter jet armed with a deadly French-made missile and that there would be a repeat of an attack on the ship as happened two years before to a sister ship. The data from all the instruments clearly indicated by speed, size and elevation, that this was not a fast deadly war plane heading towards them, but rather, an innocuous civil airliner making its routine flight. But, as the seconds ticked away and the aircraft drew closer and closer to the ship, the imagination of the commander got out of control. Fear took over from logic. Then followed the illogical order to shoot down the harmless civil jet liner The uncontrollable did its work.

This uncontrollable element in our make-up flits through the mind, pulling out drawers of memory, rushing through the heart and literally causing palpitations. It can be an expert at distortion, perverting the thoughts about God, about ourselves, and about others. By nature it plays with truth and the results are falsehood and the myriad actions on the part of people individually and as nations one to another, which in retrospect seem so illogical It is not for nothing that imagination is used in Scripture in the first book of God's remedial revelation to man.

When the Flood waters abated, Noah offered a sacrifice of worship to God. We are told that the terror of cosmic physical judgment would not come on the world again in this form. How could this be without God's honour being impugned by the recurring and increasing evil that keeps the world from happiness and righteousness right up to the present day as we begin the third millenium? The answer is that God had another way of mercy in his covenant by which his law would be fulfilled and given a three-fold dimension, where the creation force behind the design of God the Father is synchronised to the spiritual aspiration and acknowledgment of his created people, by the new agency of His only Begotten Son. By the efficacy of the work of Christ as the mediator of the new covenant based on Divine Love, crucified but triumphant, the power of the Resurrection opens heaven to those who were strangers, and the breath of the Spirit has brought the new life of overflowing joy, redeeming joy to their souls. Doubts have no place here; the shadows of fear even of death are dispelled by light, glorious light; sin is vanquished.

The soul bathes in the *fountain opened ...for sin and uncleanness.* (Zechariah 13:1) The blessings are possessed by faith, for all this is spiritual and stamped with the insignia of heaven. Until man appropriates this by faith, the imagination of man is out of control, a runaway. But in a moment we can be part of the picture of God's mercy. Then we are listed as God's people, the poor people who are rich spiritually; the people whose minds and hearts and souls are replenished from heaven daily as we seek the Lord; a people who are blessed with an inner and enduring peace for their minds are stayed upon God and filled with the ordered sequences of reasonable consequences -- the consequences of living in communion with God, and abiding within the law of Christ and loving others in the giving out of ourselves in different forms of service. Listen to Scripture.

> *And the Lord said in his heart, I will not again curse the ground any more for man's sake;*
>
> *For the imagination of man's heart is evil from his youth; neither will I smite any more everything living, as I have done.*

(Genesis 8:21)

Having Christ on the bridge with you

No longer is the imagination uncontrolled and vulnerable to all kinds of guilt thoughts, fears, suspicion, false schemes of success, vain propositions of happiness, intimidation by bullies or threats by those in positions of power. Now there is a kind of nonchalance. You have a part in the saving contract with the Most High, the Almighty. Your mind is now filled with the mighty promises of God, which are Yea and Amen in Christ Jesus.(See 2 Corinthians 1:20) You know him in whom you have believed.(See 2 Timothy 1:12) Your mind is stayed on him; you live now, looking unto Jesus the author and the finisher of your faith. God is for you, so who can be against you!

That is what the psalmist and Isaiah and all the prophets and apostles are telling us in the Scriptures. And when the Spirit comes into your heart, and you hear him whispering in a still small voice of assurance that he is aboard, on the bridge behind you as you look at your compass and keep a steady hand on the wheel-- well, you are at peace. You are no longer at the mercy of all the unknowns. Your mind is occupied with heavenly thoughts and filled to overflowing with wonder at the love that found you and the glory that awaits you at journey's end. Isn't this a way to live? Turn to the Lord; come with God's people and feed upon the Bread of life. Let your mind be stayed upon God and peace like a river, a tranquil river will flow through your whole being.

The calm of inward peace

Now the shadows, the terrors, the disturbing forebodings, the haunting reminders of the sins of our youth, are all gone. In their place there is peace. All is reconciled through Christ and his atonement. From being full of the uncontrollable, which we all know as a potent negative within us as a driving force, distorting truths about God, about ourselves, about other people, giving us to be prisoners of prejudice, rather than agents of dynamic truth, we are changed. All the problems of life no longer crowd in on us; other people no longer appear a threat to us; God himself is no longer someone we have to reckon with in the future; our failure to make the grade in righteousness, the righteousness of God, is no longer an issue. Why not? Yes, because Christ is our righteousness. And we have heeded the injunction to put our trust in the Lord and his mercy. Now the mind is tranquil, like calm waters in a bay after the storm has passed. That is a picture of grace filling our hearts. All is at peace within. Now you say as faith rest in God and his mercy, *I will both lay me down in peace, and sleep: for thou Lord, only makest me to dwell in safety.* (Psalm 4 : 8) You see, this peace permeates the whole man. This is what David commends to us, to other people. This is not just for the mind, it is also for the heart.

Pour out your heart before God

What does that mean? Surely it means that we empty ourselves unreservedly before God. It may be together in a service of common worship where the whole congregation turn to the Lord, or it may be that you go to your room or find a place alone where you cast yourself at the feet of Christ and pour out all the pent-up emotion of your heart in penitence and total surrender. I can see you now as you let go all the old affections that held you as a slave. Now they wash out with your tears. But tears will not do this. Many have often wept for their sins and were hardened only to fall and weep again and again. But God does not despise the tears of the penitent. What happens is that as our will opens the door of the heart, inwards, and Christ comes in, he brings with him such expulsive and redeeming power that all other affection is dissolved. It is neutralised. And the potential affection of our being is now redirected by the compulsion of his love. Love is awakened within us that is born of God and comes to us as we come to Christ. No one comes to Christ with a broken heart and gets turned away. Christ's great work is to heal and bring his peace. Now the heart is enraptured with the love of Christ.

Note this is not a transitory experience. Now the heart with all the agitation and stress of our uncertain life, is stilled. It quietly beats like a car whose engine runs smoothly. But we must also be realistic. There is no guarantee that the heart of the believer will be filled with joy all the time. I say this, because I also know times when my heart is troubled. It is hard to articulate what makes it so or describe the burden that makes the heart so heavy, however hard the mind tries.

One recourse we may follow is to go to a place where we are by ourselves. I recall a hill I resorted to several times, when I was resident master in a boys' School in Wester Ross, Scotland. There, looking out to the misty islands of the Hebrides, I would kneel beside a rock in the heather. There I laid my self open to the searching scrutiny of a righteous God, who is of purer eyes than to countenance iniquity. I recall letting go, emptying all my sins in confession to my high priest, Jesus the mediator of the Covenant of grace, the one who knows all our infirmities, and knows our hearts and knows our sorrows, and the one only who has the supreme power of love to forgive. There I poured out my heart before the Lord. Yes, I would call upon the Lord unreservedly to meet me there. I know that there was therapy for the soul just to do this physiologically. But there was more to it than the subjective. There was one time, when the sun broke through and came into my heart with warmth and light, and joy and spiritual health from the storehouses of grace filled my heart with melody. I recall going back down that hill in Lochalsh, renewed and revived like a new man.

Collecting our inner peace

You see, Christ gives peace to the whole man, the mind and the heart as we rest on the Lord and trust in his mercy, with the mind calmly drawing from the Word of God as a lamp to our feet and a light to our path. And every day you and I have to make time to seek the Lord to reflect and talk to our soul within us; in God's presence who hears us as we touch on our needs for forgiveness of the sins of yesterday, and the grace we need for the challenges of another day. Remember we know God overhears, and we can then turn to him and ask him in prayer. And when he opens the door to the treasures of his grace, if you look, in the holy light of his glory, you will see glorious riches for the soul, an abundance of provisions that are the resources of his people. There are comforts for sorrows, weapons for the warfare of the spirit, and the breastplate of righteousness, shoes for the road and the sword of the Word. But who can describe all the heavenly things that God reveals to the soul! How can a penitent articulate such details especially if he gets a glimpse of his Redeemer, Christ himself in all his loveliness and all his beauty. For redemptive love is found in him, in his sufferings, in his death, in his anguish and his tears. But joy fills the soul as he sees Christ as the victor, mighty to save to the uttermost and there beside the Father in his risen power, making continual intercession for us. Then he rises from his devotions, refreshed and in a real way completely invigorated. He feels that peace has pervaded his whole being and he can feel a wonderful freedom from all care. Read Paul's letter to the church at Philippi. It is full of dynamic spiritual food for you and me, describing the unique loving bonds that bind believers in the covenant of God's peace, and also in which we are guided in all the choices before us as we meet different situations each day. Now we can do anything in God's will and strengthened with might in the inner man, we can give out to others in a new spirit of confidence and tolerance, because we have caught a glimpse of the eternal resources for all who come to God in Christ's name. Now we are serene and calm, because God's Spirit gives us Christ's peace.

The peace of God which passeth all understanding shall keep your hearts and minds through Christ Jesus.

(Philippians 4:7)

When ever we think in terms of spiritual peace, we remember that Christ came to give it to us as a fulfilment of God's Word. The prophets spoke of such a day coming on earth. For us we have double blessing, we enjoy fulfilment and see prophecy confirmed. No, that is not the end and there is a Second Coming of Christ and soon for us all, there is everlasting joy when the angels will come to bring us to glory. But here our lives already become an adventure in which we are emancipated from worry, in which we have freedom within God's will, that makes our step on the longest journey of his bidding, feel light and easy. Listen to the prophet Isaiah who complements the comfort chapter of John 14.

For ye shall go out with joy, and be led forth with peace: the mountains and the hills shall break forth before you into singing, and all the trees of the field shall clap their hands. (Isaiah 55 : 12)

What more can one ask for! David calls us to trust in God,

who gives peace of mind and peace of heart. O yes, you say, but what of the soul? The answer is that the soul is within the heart. It dominates the inner being and the whole person. What God is to our souls, he ultimately is to the whole man: and what God is to the whole man, he also is to the soul.

We now have a a refuge in God

David says, **God is a refuge for us**, verse 8, that is for our whole life now and forever. This is not the provision of a local hideaway, a parochial provincial safety cell in the midst of the greatness of the created world. The refuge God provides for us takes into account all the different elements that can come to the human mind as it consciously reflects on all knowledge, natural and revealed. This is not an escape from reason. It is just that reason is not the door to this solution which is our refuge for the soul. It cannot be, for the soul corresponds to the spiritual and the heavenly and the mechanics of believing demands faith. This opens a door that is valid for all people, even the handicapped in life. All that is needed is faith. Reason then becomes developed when faith has brought us into the benefits of having God as our refuge. From the vantage point of faith, all seems different. Life is not then a problem. Much that was a puzzle is now reasonable as we think from the premise of belief in a God who is all-wise and all-powerful. A God whose mercy covers our sins with forgiving love and takes us back into communion with him, is also able to do anything that reason can think of. The reality is that faith sees what Christ has done for us. Thus faith is not a blind faith. The understanding is opened like the eyes of the blind Bartimeus who was healed by Christ. Christ is the light of the world who shines into our hearts through the windows of the sensory and the emotions. Faith demands that the will open the door and Christ comes in. The whole inner life is flooded with light. Where Christ is there is this incandescent radiance. The camera of the mind and all the emotions of the heart join with the soul in the spiritual experience of grace, as it changes our consciousness to become partakers of salvation through faith in what Christ has done. Light of understanding activates reason and the mind portrays the wonders of his redeeming work. So that we are compulsively employed as servants of God through our conviction that He is all in all to us, and the only Potentate in the universe. Therefore we join with the people of God seeking to be.

> *Strengthened with all might, according to his glorious power, unto all patience and long-suffering with joyfulness;*
>
> *Giving thanks unto the Father, which hath made us meet to be partakers of the inheritance of the saints in light:*
>
> *Who hath delivered us from the power of darkness and hath translated us into the kingdom of his dear Son;*
>
> *In whom we have redemption through his blood, even the forgiveness of sins;*
>
> *Who is the image of the invisible God, the first-born of every creature.*

(Colosssians 1: 11 - 15)

The Anglican, John Henry Newman, who surprised the ecclesiastical world by becoming a Roman Catholic, loved to dwell upon Christ as light. Perhaps that is why he used light as a synonym for Christ in his hymn *Lead Kindly Light.* In a sermon while he was still at St Mary's, the university church at Oxford, he preached on Psalm 27:4. The sermon is on the devotional life as it maintains communion with God. Newman points out that arguing by reason has no premise from which to proceed to make deductions or come to conclusions. He suggests that man has first to **act** instead of **arguing**. Is he not pointing to the key to right thinking? **Faith is an act,** a real dynamic action, an action that activates God-power and brings into gear the dynamics of redemptive power into our beings. Faith gives us the spiritual power; reason observes and studies the technology of the spiritual workings of God, in the heart, in the church, in the world and also muses with a joyous delight as it follows faith in reaching upwards and beyond to the realms of glory and light in the life to come which God has prepared for them that love him.

Faith brings the light of Christ to the understanding. Reason then inductively traces the power through the network of the intricate mechanism of creation, in all the varied fields of knowledge. No one man can do this in his life. The main thing is that reason operates on the principle of faith. Faith brings the light of God's solution to our lives so that it is like a torch for the mind to make its observations with spiritual understanding. Reason can then be the means of enhancing and magnifying the Name of Christ and glorifying God. For it sees more and more of the wonders He has done in the myriad aspects of the created world which we all are privileged to see in part, even on the nature programs brought to our television screens. And at the end of the day, no mind even that of the Newtons or the Einsteins, has ever grasped the uncharted avenues of existence in the astrophysical or the spiritual dimensions. What can be said to every human being is this that when God is your refuge, nothing hostile, in the world we know nor the world we do not know can ever touch you. God has spoken in creation; God has spoken in revelation. All power is given to Christ in heaven and in earth.

If all got down on their knees, rulers and people, like ancient Nineveh in humbling penitence, in symbolic 'sackcloth and ashes', praising God and asking for a manifestation of his saving power, something would happen! Great things would happen. If we pause in the rush of life, and the whole community joins in, let it be on any scale, God knows about it. He is near.

It is not his will that thousands die because man fights against man, or abuses the stewardship of the earth, so that disease like cancer and aids among all the others, reduce society to an industry of neurotics, obsessed with self-preservation.

If a visitor did come to visit our planet earth, he would really be puzzled to find the contradictions. On the one hand he could see the signs of spiritual aspiration in the churches and the books and the cemeteries. On the other hand, he could also see the evidence of fear of our fellow man as the dominating drive in expending human energy and the primary avenue of implementing knowledge. Did you know that nations claim first choice for all inventions by any citizen, and the military have the prerogative to us it solely for war against other nations. Fear is the driving force of our society, insecurely trying to find a hidingplace from the threatening forces that the mind conceives and is continually alarmed about and afraid of. Man is really running away from himself. He is hiding in the sand, afraid of self-knowledge. For self-knowledge brings in the factors of failure, of finite power, of accountability to the Creator, of evasive reaction to the overtures of mercy, the indictment of moral law and the ever-recurring uncertainty that all the fabric of man's genius and all the structures of his humanist hopes may come crashing down like a tower of Babel, or dissolve in a molecular dissolution of *fervent heat.* (2nd Peter 3 : 10)

What we see in the Word of God, is that God has found a way out of the human dilemma. It is a redeeming way by which we find refuge, an everlasting refuge in Christ. This is God's way. This is where you will find multitudes who rest on the promises of God and live by faith in the Son of God. On Christ rests the destiny of mankind. He is the fulcrum where death in conterbalanced by life; where judgement is outweighed by mercy; where the forces of fear and hate, are cancelled out by the **dynamic power of elective love**.

God's Rescue ship

David wants the world to know that God is a refuge, like a great ship that comes along to a disaster scene. You can keep filling this ship, rescuing as many as you like, pulling them in from the storm-tossed seas of life where the waves threaten to separate them from the flimsy rafts or leaky lifeboats, and yet there is room. Just think of it. No wonder there is heard in the dwellingplace of the righteous, the song of melody of joy and health. They have fled for refuge to Christ and laid hold on the claims of redeeming love, and nothing in the world here or the world to come can ever touch them with harm. They enjoy peace here and as they think of the tomorrows, they anticipate the glory that awaits the people of God, who live for him here and honour his law. Hear David, *Come and hear, all ye that fear God, and I will declare what he hath done for my soul.* (Psalm 66: 16)

For those who do not make the grade

Here is a testimony by a very human person, for David was no paragon of virtue. History gives him a low credit rating in the scales of conventional character consistency. The fact is that he would not make the grade in the ecclesiastical jockeying for position in church nor in the moralism of the secular state. Indeed, it is likely he would be disqualified and sadly told that he was an outsider. But no one could ever keep David from being one of God's people or disqualify him from the blessings of a merciful God. He knew that he forfeited many privileges because of his sins. But there is an incomparable disposition of penitence, an overwhelming portrayal of contrition by David which makes him a role model, not for the smart spiritual saints, but for those who fell into sin, who were tempted and sinned, who were naive or blinded by Satan and sinned. Do you see what this means? The sinners of this world, those who haven't a leg to stand on spiritually, the outcasts, those who are lost, who have no safe smug security in conventional formal privileged psychological or ecclesiastical securities, have here a refuge specially designed by the architect of the universe, just for them.

The building principle of mercy

This refuge is built on the principle of mercy. Hear the Psalmist as he turns to talk with God in the last verse.

Also unto thee, O Lord, belongeth mercy.

Because mercy is unsinkable, it is a substance whose spiritual texture defies analysis in the laboratories of the priests of our supposed sophisticated day, dressed not in black coats, but in white overalls. The buoyancy of mercy never fails, those who didn't make the grade like David can never sink. You see, this refuge is provided by God. This testimony is not just for what God has done for one man, but what God has done for all mankind.

'Come,' he says, 'and hear this.' The tone is spiritual and it is personal. After all we are all persons. David speaks for you and me, saying, 'God has brought my soul out of the dark depths in the inner life with all it self-loathing; its shame for my sins; its uncontrollable imaginings of failure, of suspicion of fear, of pessimism. He has brought my soul to life, so that it has become loosed from the earthly, the negative, and defeatist. Now my soul lives with an animation that comes from heaven, I have a life which intensifies the mortal, so that life is more abundant, with overtones and connotations of the eternal, bound up in the hopes that rest on the covenant promises of God which endure forever.'

Changing the negatives of life into positives

The soul has a liberty which shrinks the significance of all earthly circumstances because nothing can suppress the visitations of the Spirit, however dark is the prison or hard the circumstances of oppression. Even the walls of mis-understanding, of spite, of resentment, of being sent to coventry for not making the grade in the system, and thus being deprived of the fellowship which the soul longs for, somehow no longer project themselves as the negative forces that keep us from blessings, but become positive expedients, by which we are driven into a closer fellowship with God and therefore enjoy at first hand the dynamic experience of his grace.

The thread of testimony runs through the whole of Scripture, spelling out what God has done and what he can do for me and you. All the writers in Scripture strike this note.

What God does for the soul.

David tells us that God becomes our refuge. He is quite emphatic; we cannot **hedge our bets** as we are exhorted to do in the ways of the world. God rejects that superstitous response, though we try and buy our salvation with a million dollars and get our name engraved in the stone walls of a cathedral. Listen to the psalmist in this psalm, this soliloquy in which he talks to himself, in which he speaks to God, and invites us all to find our refuge in God.

> **Trust in God at all times, my people.**
> **Tell him all your troubles, for he is our**
> **refuge.**
>
> **Men are like a puff of breath;**
> **great and small alike are worthless.**
> **Put them on the scales, and they weigh**
> **nothing;**
> **they are lighter than a mere breath.**
>
> **Don't put your trust in violence;**

> **don't hope to gain anything by robbery;**
> **even if your riches increase,**
> **don't depend on them.**(verse 8 - 10)NEB

Attending the last great party

This means that we let go of every other refuge or security for our soul and rest in the provision of heaven, in the covenant that endures for ever, that of redeeming grace through the merits of Jesus Christ. You meet a great variety of people in the fellowship of those who have God as their refuge. Sadly we may have to wait until the gates of glory open to see many of them, because of all the divisive influences that separate the people of God from the fellowship of one another. We know that there will be some from all walks of life, presidents, politicians, teachers, scientists, butchers, bakers, engineers, fishermen, nurses, soldiers, cooks, captains, miners, horse-trainers, carpenters, prostitutes, masons, painters, physcians boxers shopkeepers, printers, welders, policemen, jockeys soldiers, sailors, airmen, receptionists, farmers, opticians, pilots, golfers and many more. But that tells us only what people do. Those who will be at the last great party are there because of what God, in Christ, has done in carrying out his redemptive will on the Cross of Calvary as a historic fact. Those who are members of the covenant of grace have come face to face with self-knowledge of what they are in the presence of God's holiness. You realise that God does not judge as man judges. The description then of those who are God's people, is indicated throughout Scripture. Those aboard the Ark of Mercy are called the meek and poor, the halt and the maimed, the naked and the blind, the humble and the contrite, the penitent and the persecuted, the blessed and the broken-hearted, the selfless and the self-sacrificing. There a common denominator in that they are in God's sight called the 'righteous.' And this is so because they are saved by grace, forgiven through the Shed

Blood of the Lamb, the Son of God. You wonder and think, What a crowd of hypochondriacs with so many negatives of personality!   That is where you make a big mistake. All of these have fled for refuge to Christ. In him and through him every negative is changed into a positive; every deficiency is compensated a hundred fold. They are a transformed people. It is true that this does not appear to be complete while they are in this life, but when you see them in glory, you too, yourself, will have to be there to be part of this, **the last great party,** you also will have to be transformed. Then the power of the love of Christ that gives sinners the rights of kings to an inheritance of the saints in light, and the privileges of priests offering their lives as a well-pleasing sacrifice to God, will pervade the great company of the redeemed, like a perfume, the exotic spiritual holiness which lingers forever about those whose life is hidden from the earthly, in Christ their Lord. And that is life for ever more.

My soul, wait thou with patience
upon thy God alone;
On him dependeth all my hope
and expectation.

He only my salvation is,
and my strong rock is he;
He only is my sure defence:
I shall not moved be.

In God my glory placed is,
and my salvation sure;
In God the rock is of my strength,
my refuge most secure.

Ye people, place your confidence
in him continually;
Before him pour ye out your heart;
God is our refuge high.

(Psalm 62 : 5 - 8 Scottish Psalter)

...And they shall teach no more every man his neighbour, and every man his brother, saying Know the Lord; for they shall all know me, from the least of them unto the greatest of them, saith the Lord; for I will forgive their iniquity, and I will remember their sins no more.

Jeremiah 31, v. 4

Books in this Series

A Dream Come True
Psalm 126

Shopping for the Soul
Psalm 1
Psalm 32
Psalm 33
Psalm 65

The Cape of Joy
Psalm 3
Psalm 39
Psalm 41
Psalm 102

A Pillar of Faith
Psalm 2
Psalm 62

All books availablefrom the Catalone Press
P.O. Box 1878, Sydney, NS B1P 6W4 Canada